Ibn Qayyim a

Patience and Gratitude

An abridged translation of
'Uddat as-sabirin wa dhakhirat ash-shakirin

Translated by: Nasiruddin al-Khattab

Ta-Ha Publishers Ltd.
www.taha.co.uk

Copyright © Ta-Ha Publishers Ltd. 1997

First Published in Dhu'l-Qa'dah 1417AH/March 1997CE
Reprinted 1997, 1998, 2000, 2001, 2003, 2004, 2005, 2007, 2009, 2012, 2015

Published by:
Ta-Ha Publishers Ltd.
Unit 4, Windsor Centre, London, SE27 9NT
Website: www.taha.co.uk
E-mail: sales@taha.co.uk

By: Ibn Qayyim al-Jawziyyah
Translated by: Nasiruddin al-Khattab
Edited by: Abdassamad Clarke

British Library Cataloguing in Publication Data
Patience and Gratitude
I. al-Jawziyyah, Ibn Qayyim

ISBN-13: 978 1 89794061 7

Printed and bound by: Imak Ofset, Turkey

Cover Photo by Shakir Cadir
Design and Typeset by: Shakir Cadir .: www.OpenSquares.co.uk

Contents

5

Translator's Introduction

We live in an era of overwhelming Western influence where two major ideas are upheld and promoted. One of these is the expectation of instant gratification, whereby few people are prepared to wait, or work hard, or suffer temporary hardship, to get results. People see a world of wealth and power, depicted on TV and in the movies, and they want it, now. Immediate satisfaction is expected in this world, so how much harder must it be for such people to think in terms of preparing themselves for the Hereafter!

The other major idea promoted by Western influences is the cult of the superman. Here, too, TV and movies must take much of the blame for filling people's minds with the notion that the stronger and wealthier you are, the freer you are to do what you like, regardless of the consequences. The idea of the "survival of the fittest" is used to justify destroying the weak. In their quest for independence and superiority, the godless are turning this world into a living hell where competition and conflict prevail. Crime is on the increase, as religion and morality are no longer deterrent forces, and a sense of fear and insecurity is spreading in its wake. Mental illness and psychological disorders are a further symptom of the malaise caused by negative Western influences.

The Islamic way is in sharp contrast to the current trends of the West. Our Creator knows best the make-up of the human psyche, and the guidance of the Qur'an and Sunnah is in perfect harmony with human nature. Not for nothing is Islam known as *din al-fitrah* (the life-transaction of the natural state of man). Muslim scholars and scientists developed an extensive and deep knowledge of human behaviour and psychology, which was firmly rooted in the guidance of the Qur'an and Sunnah. Centuries ago, scholars developed Islamic concepts by which any person

seek kbmic guidance as it is Din of fitrah

6

who is seeking strength of willpower, and perfection may be guided. Instead of struggling alone, for no other reason than self-gratification, Islam channels us into seeking perfection for the sake of Allah, and teaches us to seek His help in doing so. Thus we have important Islamic ideals such as: *'ubudiyyah* (being a true slave of Allah), which puts a person in touch with the highest Power in this universe, the Power of Allah; *tawakkul* (putting one's trust in Allah), concerning which the Prophet ﷺ advised, "Whoever wishes to be the strongest among men, let him put his complete trust in Allah"; and *sabr* (patience, forbearance, fortitude), which enables a man to face hardship with dignity and to accept times of ease without becoming arrogant.

Ibn Qayyim al-Jawziyyah (1292-1350 CE) was one of these scholars. His full name was Muhammad ibn Abi Bakr ibn Ayyub ibn Sa'd az-Zar'i and his *kunya* was Abu Abdullah Shams al-Din, but he is better known as Ibn Qayyim al-Jawziyyah. Born in Damascus, Syria, he was the son of the attendant *(qayyim)* of the school of al-Jawziyyah. He lived during a period of great turmoil in the Muslim world, which was still reeling from the Mongol onslaughts. At the same time, his was an era of remarkable scholarship. He studied under the great scholar, Ibn Taymiyyah, and was also a contemporary of Ibn Kathir and others.

The present text is an abridged translation of Ibn al-Qayyim's famous work, *'Uddat as-Sabirin wa Dhakhirat ash-Shakirin* (literally, *The Equipment of the Patient and the Investment of the Grateful*). This work deals with the closely-related topics of patience and gratitude. Although often translated as "patience", the Arabic word *sabr* has a broader and deeper meaning than the English. Depending on the context, it may mean fortitude, patience, equanimity, forbearance, patient endurance, etc. *Shukr* may be translated as "gratitude" or "thankfulness". As is shown in the book, patience and gratitude are two sides of the same coin, closely-related attitudes which the Muslim should seek to foster in every aspect of his or her life.

Don't limit Islam to ibadah only – it is wider than that.

This kind of practical spiritual advice is something that today's Muslims so desperately need. Far from being a set of empty rituals and nit-picking legal technicalities, or a set of words to be repeated or chanted *ad nauseam*, Islam is a holistic way of life; if it is applied only partially, imbalance will result. A most important aspect of Islam, which must always accompany the formal "rituals" and the recitation *of du'as* and *dhikr*, is constant remembrance of Allah and constant contact with the Divine. Developing a truly Islamic attitude of patience will enable us to achieve this.

Although his works were written over six centuries ago, Ibn al-Qayyim has much to offer the modern reader. Caught as we are between the tempting influences of the West and the hidebound superstitions of some of our own Muslim communities, Ibn al-Qayyim's level-headed and above all practical advice will point us back towards a purer Islamic way, insha'Allah.

DON'T FOCUS ON SELF, BUT OUR CREATOR

It is my firm belief that Islam has the answer to many of the psychological problems that trouble mankind today, such as anxiety, depression, lack of confidence, addictions, etc. In direct contrast to the Western focus on the "self", Islam tells us to look beyond ourselves and focus on Allah. By doing so, we will move towards fulfilling the purpose for which we were created, and thus attain peace with our Creator and within ourselves. This book will, insha'Allah, bring the spiritual and psychological benefits of our Islamic heritage to Muslims who do not have access to the works of scholars in the original Arabic.

Nasiruddin al-Khattab
December 1996

Rules of life

1. ABAD (SLAVE). 2. SABAR 3. SHUKAR.
4. TAWAKUL. 5. CONSTANT remembrance
6. CONSTANT CONTACT

Translator's Note

Translations of Qur'anic quotations have been adapted from the translation by Yusuf Ali. However the archaic style of the translator has been modernised, so that "thou" has been changed to "you", "doeth" to "does", etc.

Abbreviations of the blessings customarily pronounced by Muslims following the names of the Prophet and *Sahabah* are used in the text, as follows:

ﷺ is *salla'llahu 'alaihi wa sallam* (may Allah bless him and grant him peace), following mention of the Prophet Muhammad ﷺ;
ؓ / ؓ / ؓ are *radiy'allahu 'anhu/ 'anha/ 'anhum* (may Allah be pleased with him/her/them), after the name of a Companion or wife of the Prophet ﷺ.

Finally, a note on gender usage: although the text of this book tends to use the masculine (he, him) in describing human situations, this is in no way intended to exclude female readers. This use of the masculine reflects the Arabic usage, where - grammatically speaking - the masculine may always include the feminine, as in *al-Muslimun* (masculine plural), which can include female as well as male Muslims. Repeated use of "he or she" or "him or her" would have made the language of the book very stilted and tedious to read. The advice and suggestions given by Ibn Qayyim al-Jawziyyah may be understood to apply equally to males and females.

Author's Prologue

Praise be to Allah, the Patient *(as-Sabur)*, the Thankful *(ash-Shakur)*, the Most High *(al-'Aliyy)*, the Greatest *(al-Kabir)*, the All-Hearing *(as-Sami)*, the All-Seeing *(al-Basir)*, the All-Knowing *(al-'Alim)*, the All-Powerful *(al-Qadir)*, Whose Power controls every single creature and Whose Will dominates every single event. His Call to people to prepare for the Hereafter has been made so strongly that even the dead could hear it. I bear witness that there is no god except Allah, and I bear witness that Muhammad is His Slave and Messenger, the best of His creation who did not spare any effort to advise this *Ummah*, the most patient in accepting the decree of Allah and the most grateful for His blessings. Truly he conveyed the Message of Allah and proclaimed the Truth, and endured in the way of Allah that which no human being had ever endured. He followed Allah's commands patiently and gratefully, until he gained the pleasure of Allah and attained the highest degree of patience, such as had never before been reached.

Patience, or patient perseverance, is obligatory, according to the consensus of the scholars, and it is half of faith *(iman)*, the other half of which is gratitude *(shukr)*. Patience is mentioned in the Qur'an around ninety times. The relation of patience to *iman* is like the relation of the head to the body, and the one who has no patience has no *iman*. Allah has commanded patience for the Believers in the following *ayah*:

> *"O you who believe! Seek help with patient perseverance* (sabr) *and prayer..."* (al-Baqarah 2:153)

Patience has also been made a condition for a person's entering Paradise and being saved from Hellfire; on the Day of Judgement Allah will say:

10

"I have rewarded them this day for their patience and constancy (patience): they are indeed the ones that have achieved bliss..." (al-Mu'minun 23:111)

And Allah commended the patient (those who have patience) when He said:
"...(it is righteousness...) to be firm and patient, in pain or suffering and adversity, and throughout all periods of panic. Such are the people of truth, the God-fearing." (al-Baqarah 2:177)

"...Allah loves those who are firm and steadfast." (Al 'Imran 3:146)

Allah has told us that He is with those who have patience; this is a special "companionship" *(ma'iyyah)* which means that He is protecting and supporting them, which is over and above the ordinary "companionship" which applies to believers and disbelievers alike whereby Allah has knowledge of them and is watching over them. Allah has told us:
"...And be patient and persevering: for Allah is with those who patiently persevere." (al-Anfal 8:47)

The Prophet ﷺ told us that patience is all good and full of goodness, and said that, "There is no gift better than patience." 'Umar ibn al-Khattab ﷺ said, "The best days of our lives were ours by virtue of patience."

This book has been written to highlight the urgent need for patience, and to explain that our happiness in this life and our salvation in the Hereafter depend on patience. This book is filled with benefits and readers will benefit from its advice and teachings. What is good and correct in this book is by the help of Allah, and what is mistaken in it is from the Shaytan. May Allah forgive the author and the editor. Allah is the Greatest Helper, and we put our trust in Him.

· Happiness & Patience ·

CHAPTER I

The Definition of Patience

Sabr is an Arabic word which comes from a root meaning to detain, refrain and stop. There is an expression in Arabic, "so-and-so was killed *sabran*", which means that he was captured and detained until he died. In the spiritual sense, patience means to stop ourselves from despairing and panicking, to stop our tongues from complaining, and to stop our hands from striking our faces and tearing our clothes at times of grief and stress.

What scholars have said about patience

Some scholars have defined patience as a good human characteristic or a positive psychological attitude, by virtue of which we refrain from doing that which is not good. Human beings cannot live a proper, healthy life without patience.

Abu 'Uthman said, "The one who has patience is the one who has trained himself to handle difficulties." Amr ibn 'Uthman al-Makki said, "Patience means to keep close to Allah and to accept calmly the trials He sends, without complaining or feeling sad." Al-Khawwas said, "Patience means to adhere to the rules of the Qur'an and Sunnah." Another scholar said, "Patience means to refrain from complaining." 'Ali ibn Abi Talib ﷺ said, "Patience means to seek Allah's help."

Is it better to have patience at a time of difficulty, or to be in a situation which does not require patience?

Abu Muhammad al-Hariri said, "Patience means not seeing any difference between times of ease and times of hardship, and being content at all times." I (Ibn Qayyim) say this is too difficult, and we are not instructed to be like this. Allah has created us in such a way that we feel the difference between times of ease and times of hardship, and all that we can do is refrain from panicking at times of stress. Patience does not mean feeling the same at both easy and difficult times. That is beyond us, and is not part of our nature. Having an easy time is better for us than having a difficult time. As the Prophet ﷺ said in his well-known *du'a*, "If You are not angry with me, then I do not care what happens to me, but still I would rather have Your blessings and favour." This does not contradict the hadith which says, "No-one has ever been given a better gift than patience", because that refers to a time after a test or trial has befallen a person. But ease is still better.

Patience and **Shakwah** *(complaint)*

Shakwah (complaint) falls into two categories: The first type means to complain to Allah, and this does not contradict patience. It is demonstrated by several of the Prophets, for example, when Ya'qub عليه السلام said:

> *"I only complain of my distraction and anguish to Allah."* (Yusuf 12:86)

Earlier, Ya'qub عليه السلام had said *"sabrun Jamil"*, which means "patience is most fitting for me". The Qur'an also tells us about Ayyub عليه السلام:

> *"And (remember) Ayyub (Job), when he cried to his Lord, 'Truly distress has seized me...'"* (al-Anbiya 21:83)

The epitome of patience, the Prophet ﷺ, prayed to his Lord, "O Allah, I complain to You of my weakness and helplessness." Musa عليه السلام prayed to Allah, saying, "O Allah, all praise is due to You, and complaint is made only to You, and You are the only One from Whom we seek help and in Whom we put our trust, and there is no power except by Your help." The second type of complaint involves complaining to people, either directly, through our words, or indirectly, through the way we look and behave. This is contradictory to patience.

Opposing forces

Psychologically speaking, every person has two forces at work within him or her. One is the "driving force", which pushes him towards some actions, and the other is the "restraining force", which holds him back from others. Patience essentially harnesses the driving force to push us towards good things, and the restraining force to hold us back from actions that may be harmful to ourselves or others.

Some people have strong patience when it comes to doing what is good for them, but their patience is weak with regard to restraint from harmful actions, so we may find that a person has enough patience to perform acts of worship *(salah, sawm, Hajj)*, but has no patience in controlling himself and refraining from following his whims and desires, and in this way he may commit *haram* deeds. Conversely, some people may have strong patience in abstaining from forbidden deeds, but their patience in obeying commandments and performing *'ibadah* is too weak. Some people have no patience in either case! And, needless to say, the best people are those who possess both types of patience.

So, a man may have plenty of patience when it comes to standing all night in prayer, and enduring whatever conditions of heat or cold may be prevalent, but have no patience at all when it comes to lowering his gaze and refraining from looking at women. Another may have no problem in controlling his gaze, but he lacks the patience which would make him enjoin the good and forbid the evil, and he is so weak and helpless that he cannot strive against the *kuffar* and *mushrikun*. Most people will be lacking in patience in any one case, and a few lack it in all cases.

Further definition of patience

A scholar said, "To have patience means that one's common sense and religious motives are stronger than one's whims and desires." It is natural for people to have an inclination towards their desires, but common sense and the religious motive should limit that inclination. The two forces are at war: sometimes reason and religion win, and sometimes whims and desires prevail. The battlefield is the heart of man.

Patience has many other names, according to the situation. If patience consists of restraining sexual desire, it is called honour, the opposite of which is adultery and promiscuity. If it consists of controlling one's stomach, it is called self-control, the opposite of which is greed. If it consists of keeping quiet about that which it is not fit to disclose, it is called discretion, the opposite of which is disclosing secrets, lying, slander or libel. If it consists of being content with what is sufficient for one's needs, it is called abstemiousness, the opposite of which is covetousness. If it consists of controlling one's anger, then it is called forbearance, the opposite of which is impulsiveness and hasty reaction. If it consists of refraining from haste, then it is called gracefulness and steadiness, the opposite of which is to be hot-headed. If it consists of refraining from running away, then it is called courage, the opposite of which is cowardice. If it consists of refraining from taking revenge, then it is called forgiveness, the opposite of which is revenge. If it consists of refraining from being stingy, then it is called generosity, the opposite of which is miserliness. If it consists of refraining from being lazy and helpless, then it is called dynamism and initiative. If it consists of refraining from blaming and accusing other people, then it is called chivalry (*muru'ah*, literally "manliness").

Different names may be applied to patience in different situations, but all are covered by the idea of patience. This shows that Islam in its totality is based on patience.

Is it possible to obtain the quality of patience?
If a person does not naturally possess the characteristic of patience, he can attain this characteristic by acting as if he does possess it, until it eventually becomes second nature. This is what the Prophet 鬆 has told us in the hadith, "Whoever tries to be patient, then Allah will help

him to be patient." A person can also strive to control his sexual desire and lower his gaze until these too become second nature. The same applies to all other desirable characteristics such as steadiness, generosity and courage.

CHAPTER 2

Different Perspectives on Patience

Patience may be of two types, either physical or psychological, and both types may either be by choice, or without choice, as follows:

1. Physical patience by choice, such as doing hard labour willingly.
2. Physical patience without choice, such as patiently bearing illness, beatings and extremes of heat and cold.
3. Psychological patience by choice, such as refraining from things which both the *Shari'ah* and common sense say are wrong.
4. Psychological patience without choice, such as patiently bearing an enforced separation from one whom you love.

Different degrees of patience

As mentioned above, patience is of two types, by choice or without choice. Patience by choice is of a higher status than patience without choice, as the latter is common to all people, but the former is not attainable by all. Therefore the patience of Yusuf 🕊 in disobeying the wife of al-Aziz, and his patience in bearing the resulting punishment, is of a higher status than his patience in response to his brothers' actions, when they threw him in the well, separated him from his father and sold him as a slave. This superior, voluntary patience is the patience of the Prophets, of Ibrahim 🕊, Musa 🕊, Nuh 🕊, 'Isa 🕊 and the Seal of the Prophets, Muhammad 🕊. Their patience was in calling people to Allah and in striving against the enemies of Allah.

The patience of men and the patience of animals

These four types of patience apply only to human beings. Animals share only the two types of patience in which there is no choice, and man is distinguished by having the patience in which there is choice.

However, many people have only the types of patience that animals have, i.e. patience without choice.

The patience of jinn

Jinn share the quality of patience with humans, as they are responsible for their actions like humans are. They need patience to fulfil their responsibilities towards Allah the same way that we do. One might ask: are they responsible in the same way that we are, or in a different way? The answer is that with regard to matters of emotion and feelings they are responsible just as we are, and share the obligation to love for the sake of Allah and hate for Allah, to believe and have faith, to take believers for friends and unbelievers for enemies, etc. But as far as physical matters such as *ghusl*, *wudu*, washing after relieving oneself and circumcision are concerned, they are not the same as us. Their duties in that regard are in accordance with the way they are created.

The patience of angels

Another question that may arise is: Do angels have patience? The answer is that the angels are not tested with whims and desires that contradict their reason and knowledge. For them, worshipping and obeying Allah are like breathing is for us. Therefore the angels do not need patience, because patience is needed when one has conflicting motives, religion and reason opposing wrong actions, whims and desires. However, the angels may have some kind of patience which befits them and makes them persevere in doing what they were created for.

The patience of man

If a man's patience is stronger than his whims and desires, then he is like an angel, but if his whims and desires are stronger than his patience, then he is like a devil. If his desire for food, drink and sex is stronger than his patience, then he is no better than an animal.

Qatadah said, "Allah created angels with reason and no desires, animals with desires and no reason, and man with both reason and desires." So if a man's reason is stronger than his desire he is like an angel, and if his desires are stronger than his reason, then he is like an animal. A little baby has only the desire for food when he needs it, and his patience is like the patience of animals. Until he reaches an age when he can tell what is what, he has no choice. When he grows a little older and develops a desire to play, then his patience by choice will develop. He will start to know what patience means when his sexual desire develops. At the same time, his power of reasoning is also developing, but between the age when he can tell right from wrong and the age of puberty, all he can see is his own interests in this world, and what might make life good or bad. This limited view will remain until he is guided by Allah, then he will have the full picture and begin to think of his interests both in this life and the Hereafter. He will become aware of where different actions may lead, and will prepare himself for a long struggle with his desires and natural inclinations.

Different degrees of patience

The kinds of patience which relate to resisting whims and desires can be graded according to how strong and effective they are. There are three degrees of patience in this respect:

1. The motive of religion is the strongest in controlling and defeating whims and desires. This level of control can only be achieved through consistent patience, and those who reach this level are victorious in this life and in the Hereafter. They are the ones "who say, 'Our Lord is Allah'" (Fussilat 41:30). These are the ones to whom, at the moment of death, the angels say, "Fear not! ...Nor grieve! But receive the Glad Tidings of the Garden (of Bliss), that which you were promised! We are your protectors in this life and in the Hereafter" (Fussilat 41:30-31). They are the ones who enjoy the companionship of Allah, and who strive in the way of Allah. They are the ones whom Allah has guided to the exclusion of others.

2. When whims and desires prevail, the religious motive is diminished. The doomed person will surrender totally to Shaytan and his forces, who will lead him wherever they want. His relationship with them will be either one of two possibilities. Either he will become their follower and a soldier in their army, which is the case of the weak person, or Shaytan will become a weapon for him, and one of his soldiers, which is the case of the strong person who rebels against Allah. Those people are the ones whose misfortune has overtaken them, as they preferred this world to the Hereafter. The main reason for their sorry fate is that they ran out of patience. The major characteristics of these people are that they lie and cheat, indulge in wishful thinking and self-admiration, delay doing good deeds, and prefer instant gains in this world to lasting gains in the Hereafter. These are the people to whom the Prophet ﷺ referred when he said, "The helpless man is the one who follows his whims and desires, and indulges in wishful thinking."

These unfortunate people are of several types. Some of them declare war against Allah and His Messenger, trying to destroy what the Prophet ﷺ brought, pushing people away from the way of Allah, and spreading corruption on earth. Some are interested solely in their own worldly interests. Some are two-faced hypocrites who try to ingratiate themselves with everybody and gain something from every situation. Some are promiscuous, and devote their entire life to the pursuit of physical pleasure. Some, if they are warned, say that they would dearly love to repent, but find it too difficult and plead that they have no chance. Some say that Allah does not need their prayers and fasting, that they will not attain salvation by virtue of their deeds, and that they will rely on the fact that Allah is Merciful. Some of them claim that refraining from committing wrong actions is like undermining the forgiveness of Allah. Some will say, "What good could my worship do after all the wrong actions I have committed? What can help a drowning man if his fingers are above water and the rest of his body is submerged?" Some say that they will repent when death approaches...

So many excuses, all because their whims and desires control their reason, and they use their reason, in turn, to find ways of fulfilling those desires. Their reason is held prisoner by the Shaytan, and put to work to serve his evil purposes, just as Muslim prisoners-of-war may be abused by the *kafirun* and forced to look after pigs, make wine or carry the Cross. The man who suppresses his reason and puts it under the control of the enemy (Shaytan) is like one who seizes a Muslim and hands him over to the *kafirun* to imprison him.

3. There is a war that is raging between the motives of reason and religion, and the motives of whims and desires. Sometimes one prevails, sometimes the other gains the upper hand. The pattern of victories for either side varies. This is the situation in the case of most believers, who mix good deeds and bad deeds.

People's ultimate fate in the Hereafter will correspond to the three situations outlined above. Some people will enter Paradise and never enter Hell, some will enter Hell and never enter Paradise, and some will enter Hell for some time before they are admitted to Paradise.

Different strengths of patience

Some people cannot have patience without struggling and facing many difficulties. Others are able to have patience easily. The first type is like a man who wrestles with a strong man and cannot beat him without the utmost effort. The second type is like a man who wrestles with a weak man and beats him easily. Such is the war between the soldiers of *ar-Rahman* and the soldiers of Shaytan. Whoever defeats the soldiers of Shaytan can defeat Shaytan himself. 'Abdullah ibn Mas'ud narrated, "A man wrestled with one of the jinn, and beat him, then asked, 'Why are you so weak and small?' The jinn answered, 'I am very big and strong compared to the rest of the jinn.'" Someone asked 'Abdullah ibn Mas'ud, "Was that man 'Umar?" and he replied, "Who else could it have been?"

Some of the *Sahabah* said, "A believers whips the Shaytan the way a person whips his camel when he is travelling."

Ibn Abi'd-Dunya narrated from some of the *salaf* that one shaytan met with another, and asked him why he was so thin. The other shaytan replied, "Because I am with a man who mentions the name of Allah when he eats, so I cannot eat with him, and he mentions the name of Allah when he drinks, so I cannot drink with him. When he enters his home he mentions the name of Allah, so I stay outside." The first shaytan said, "But I am with a man who does not mention the name of Allah when he eats, so I eat with him. He does not mention the name of Allah when he drinks, so I drink with him. When he enters his home he does not mention the name of Allah, so I enter with him."

So whoever develops the habit of patience is feared by his enemies, and whoever finds patience difficult is in danger, as his enemy will readily dare to attack him and do him harm.

When patience is needed
Patience is required in the following areas of life:
1. In worshipping Allah and following His commands;
2. In abstaining from wrong actions;
3. In accepting Allah's decree and ruling (*qada' wa qadr*). This is the advice given by Luqman when he told his son:
    "O my son! Establish regular prayer, enjoin what is just and forbid what is wrong; and bear with patient constancy whate'er betide you; for this is firmness (of purpose) in (the conduct of) affairs."
    (Luqman 31:17)

Enjoining what is just includes doing good oneself, and forbidding what is wrong includes abstaining from wrong action oneself.

Patience in worshipping Allah

Patience in worshipping Allah and carrying out His instructions means that you perform the prescribed acts of worship regularly, and do so sincerely and with knowledge. Worship that is not performed regularly is of no value. Even if worship is performed regularly, there are two dangers. Firstly, we risk losing our sincerity, if the motive for performing prayers is not to please Allah and draw closer to Him. So to protect our worship we must make sure that we are sincere. Secondly, we must be sure never to deviate from the way of the Prophet ﷺ, so we have to ensure that our worship is done according to the Sunnah.

Patience in abstaining from wrong action

This type of patience can be achieved through the fear of the punishment which follows the wrong action, or through a feeling of *haya'* (shyness or shame) before Allah for using His blessings in committing wrong actions. That feeling of *haya'* before Allah can be strengthened through learning more about Allah and knowing more about His names and attributes. *Haya'* is a characteristic of people who are noble and possess good qualities, so the person who refrains from wrong action because of *haya'* is better than the one who abstains because of fear. *Haya'* indicates that a person is mindful of Allah and His might. The person whose deterrent is the fear of Allah has his thoughts focused on the punishment. The person whose deterrent is *haya'* has his thoughts focused on Allah Himself. The fearful person's main concern is himself and how to save himself from punishment, whereas the "shy" person's main concern is Allah and His Glory. Both have attained the status of *iman*, but the "shy" person has attained *ihsan*, a higher status of *iman*, in which he conducts himself as if he can see Allah, and so his heart is filled with *haya'*.

The reason why it is so important for a believer to abstain from wrong action is because he must protect his *iman*, as wrong action decreases *iman* or extinguishes it. The Prophet ﷺ said, "When the adulterer commits adultery he is not a believer, and when the wine-imbiber drinks alcohol he is not a believer, and when the thief steals he is not a believer. The believer should abstain from many permitted actions in case they may lead to that which is forbidden."

Patience at times of trial and adversity

Patience during difficult times may be achieved by:

1. thinking of the good reward that lies ahead. The more you believe in the rewards that are waiting for you, the easier it becomes to have patience. If it were not for the anticipation of the rewards, no goals or objectives pertaining to this life or the Hereafter would have been achieved. Human nature loves instant gratification, but reason and maturity make us think of the long term outcome, which helps to strengthen our patience in enduring whatever faces us, whether there is no choice or otherwise;

2. expecting and hoping for a time of ease. This hope in itself offers a measure of immediate relief;

3. thinking of Allah's countless blessings. When we realise that we cannot enumerate the blessings of Allah, it becomes easier for us to exercise patience in facing the current adversity, because the present troubles are like a raindrop compared to the vast ocean of Allah's blessings and favours;

4. thinking of previous blessings of Allah. This will remind us of Allah's care, and strengthen our hopes and expectations of a time of ease to come.

CHAPTER 3

Five Categories of Patience

Patience can also be divided into categories following the five categories of deeds, namely *wajib* (obligatory), *mandub* (encouraged), *mahdhur* (forbidden), *makruh* (disliked) and *mubah* (permissible).

Obligatory (wajib) patience
1. Patience in abstaining from forbidden *(haram)* things and actions.
2. Patience in carrying out obligatory deeds.
3. Patience in facing adversity which is beyond one's control, such as illness, poverty, etc.

Encouraged (mandub) patience
1. Patience in abstaining from disliked *(makruh)* things.
2. Patience in performing acts of worship which are liked and encouraged *(mustahabb)*.
3. Patience in refraining from taking revenge.

Forbidden (mahdhur) patience
1. Patience in abstaining from food and drink until death.
2. Patience in abstaining from eating *haram* meat, carrion and blood, when the alternative is death from starvation. Tawus and Ahmad ibn Hanbal said, "Whoever has no choice but to eat carrion, *haram* meat and blood, but refuses to eat it and dies as a consequence, will enter Hell."
3. Patience in refraining from begging. There is a dispute as to whether begging from people is forbidden or permissible. Imam Ahmad said that this kind of patience and abstention is allowed. He was asked, "What if the person fears that if he does not do that, he will die?" Imam Ahmad answered, "No, he will not die. Allah will send him

his due provision *(rizq).*" Imam Ahmad did not allow begging: when Allah knows the need of a person and his sincerity in abstaining from begging, Allah will send him *rizq.* Other scholars, including some of Imam Ahmad's companions and Imam ash-Shafi'i said, "It is obligatory on such a person to beg, and if he did not beg, then he would be a wrongdoer, because by begging he protects himself from death."

4. Patience in enduring things that may lead to death, such as predators, snakes, fire and water.

5. Patience at times of *fitnah* when Muslims are fighting Muslims. Patience in abstaining from fighting at such a time, when Muslims are killing Muslims, is *mubah* (permissible), indeed it is *mustahabb* (liked and preferred). When the Prophet ﷺ was asked about this, he said, "Be like the better one of the two sons of Adam." In other, similar, reports he said, "Be like the slave of Allah who was killed, and not like the one who has killed," and "Let him (the killer) carry his own wrong action and your wrong action." In another report, he said, "If the sword is too bright, put your hand on your face." Allah has told us the story of the better of the two sons of Adam, and how he surrendered himself and did not fight back, and how Allah commended him for that. This is different to the case when Muslims are fighting *kafirun*: in that situation the Muslim has to defend himself, because the meaning of *jihad* is to defend himself and Islam.

Disliked (makruh) *patience*

1. Patience in abstaining from physical appetites (food, drink, sex) to the extent of causing damage to one's health.

2. Patience in doing a *makruh* deed.

Permissible (mubah) *patience*

Patience in abstaining from *mubah* deeds.

CHAPTER 4
Good Patience and Bad Patience

Bad patience means having patience in keeping away from Allah and His love and His will, because this prevents a person from fulfilling his potential of attaining perfection and doing what he was created for. This is the worst type of patience, and the most difficult, because there is no type of patience stronger than that of the person who wilfully keeps away from his Creator, as apart from Him there is no life at all. No-one is as careless as the person who has no interest in what Allah has prepared for His friends *(awliya')* in the Hereafter, that which no eye has ever seen nor ear has ever heard, and has never been imagined by any person. Once a man who admired a *zahid* (one who does without) for his *zuhd* (doing without) and lack of interest in this world said to him, "I have never seen a man who has as much *zuhd* (doing without) as you do." The *zahid* told him, "Your *zuhd is* much stronger than mine, for my *zuhd* concerns this world, and this life is short and unstable, but your *zuhd* concerns the Hereafter, which is eternal."

A man asked Shibli, "What type of patience is more difficult?" Shibli said, "Patience through seeking the help of Allah." The man said, "No." Shibli said, "Then patience for the sake of Allah." The man said, "No." Shibli said, "Patience in seeking the pleasure of Allah." The man said, "No." So Shibli asked, "What is it then?" and the man answered, "Patience in keeping away from Allah." Shibli screamed in such a way that he nearly died.

Good patience consists of two types - patience for the sake of Allah and patience by the help of Allah. Allah said:
> *"Now await in patience the command of your Lord: for verily you are in Our eyes..."* (at-Tur 52:48)

It is impossible to have patience for the sake of Allah without patience by the help of Allah:

"And be patient, for your patience is but by Allah..."
(an-Nahl 16:127)

This *ayah* tells us that patience cannot be achieved without the help of Allah, which means that in addition to the help of Allah we need the companionship of Allah, as in the hadith:

"I am his hearing with which he hears, his sight with which he sees, and his hand with which he strikes."

The help of Allah is bestowed upon the believer and the wrong-doer alike, both of whom receive blessings and *rizq*. This hadith describes something more, the companionship of Allah, which the believer will attain when he performs *nafl* (supererogatory) acts of worship until Allah loves him. When he reaches that status, and Allah is his hearing with which he hears and his seeing with which he sees, he does not move or do anything but Allah is with him. Whoever reaches this level can have patience for Allah's sake and endure severe hardship to please Him. The person who does not reach this level will not have this degree of patience; his level of patience will be in accordance with his share of Allah's companionship. The believer who enjoys Allah's companionship will reach levels of patience that are impossible for others. Those who have patience are winners in this world and the next, because Allah is with them:

"...for Allah is with those who patiently persevere."
(al-Baqarah 2:153)

Emulating the attributes of Allah
If a person loves an attribute of Allah, then this will help him to reach Him. Allah is *as-Sabur*, patient, and there is none that is more patient and forbearing than Him. It was reported that Allah revealed to Dawud 鐃, "Have My attributes, as one of My attributes is that I am

28

as-Sabur (patient)." Allah loves His attributes and characteristics, and He loves to see the effects of His attributes on His slaves. As He is Beautiful, so He loves beauty; as He is All-Forgiving, He loves forgiveness; as He is Generous, He loves generosity; as He is All-Knowing, he loves people of knowledge; as He is Strong and Powerful, so a strong believer is more beloved to Him than a weaker one; as He is *as-Sabur* (patient), so he loves those who have patience; as he is *Shakur* (grateful), so He loves those who give thanks. As He loves those who have His characteristics, so He is with them, and this is a special and unique type of companionship.

No contradiction between patience and complaining to Allah

Crying out and complaining to Allah does not mean that a person has no patience. In the Qur'an, we find Ya'qub 🕮 saying, "My course is comely patience *(sabrun jamil)*" (Yusuf 12:83), but his love and longing for his lost son Yusuf made him say, "How great is my grief for Yusuf" (Yusuf 12:83). *Sabrun jamil* refers to patience with no complaint to other people. Complaining to Allah does not cancel out patience, as Ya'qub 🕮 said, "I only complain of my distraction and anguish to Allah" (Yusuf 12:86).

Allah also enjoined *sabrun jamil* on the Prophet 🕮 and he obeyed, but he would pray, "O Allah, I complain to You of my weakness and helplessness."

CHAPTER 5

The Patience of Noble People and the Patience of Ignoble People

Every person has to exercise patience in order to face difficulties, whether he does so willingly or unwillingly. The noble person exercises patience willingly, because he realises the benefits of patience, and he knows that he will be rewarded for his patience and will be criticised if he panics. He is aware that if he does not have patience, panicking and impatience will not help him to regain missed opportunities, and will not take away things he dislikes. Whatever is decreed and is *qada' wa qadr* cannot be prevented from happening, and whatever is decreed not to happen cannot be made to happen. So an attitude of impatience and panic actually causes harm.

A wise man said, "A man with wisdom as soon as adversity appears does that which a foolish man does after a month (i.e. he resorts to patience)."

The ignoble man exercises patience only when he realises he has no choice. After wasting a lot of time and energy and panicking and struggling, he realises that his impatience will not help him. Then he exercises patience in the same way that a person who has been tied up to be whipped exercises patience.

The noble person practices patience in obeying Allah, whilst the ignoble person exercises patience in obeying the Shaytan. So ignoble people have the greatest patience in following their own whims and desires, and have the least patience in obeying their Lord. They have the greatest patience in spending in the way of Shaytan and no patience when it comes to spending even a few pennies in the way of Allah. They will endure many difficulties in order to follow their own whims and desires, but cannot bear even the least difficulties in order to please their Lord. They will endure slander for the sake of committing wrong action, but cannot exercise patience in putting up with slander for the sake of Allah. Such people will avoid enjoining the good and forbidding the evil for fear of what people will say about them for doing so, but they will expose their honour to slander and bear it most patiently for the sake of following their own whims and desires. Similarly, they are not prepared to practise patience in devoting themselves to Allah, but when it comes to devoting themselves to Shaytan and their own whims and desires, they will exercise remarkable patience. Such people will never be noble in the sight of Allah, and on the Day of Resurrection they will not be raised with the people of nobility and decency.

CHAPTER 6

Ways of Strengthening Patience

As patience is *fard* (obligatory), Allah has provided us with ways and means of obtaining and strengthening the quality of patience, for He has never instructed us to do something without providing us with help and support to do it, and ways and means of achieving it. He has never created a disease without creating a cure for it, and He has guaranteed cure when medicine is used. Even so, patience is difficult, but it is not impossible to attain. Patience consists of two elements: knowledge and action, and from these two elements are derived the remedies for all spiritual and physical troubles. Knowledge and action, combined, are always essential.

Knowledge
The element of knowledge is necessary in order to realise the benefits of following the commands of Allah and the sense of happiness and fulfilment that one may attain by following them; and to understand what it is in the forbidden things that causes harm, imperfection and evil. When a person realises that, and adds strong willpower, the desire for spiritual achievement and the wish to live as a complete human being (as opposed to an animal-like existence), then it will become easy for him to attain the quality of patience. The bitterness of patience will become sweet and the pain of patience will become joy.

Action
As we have already seen, patience is a constant battle between the motives of reason and religion on the one hand, and the motive of whims and desires on the other. If a person wants reason and religion to overcome whims and desires, then he has to strengthen the former and weaken the latter, just like promoting good health and reducing the

risk of illness. For example, a person who has a strong desire to commit adultery can take steps to combat it. He may have such a strong sexual urge that he cannot stop committing adultery; or he may not commit the act itself, but is unable to stop looking at women; or he may be able to stop looking at women but he cannot stop thinking of sex, to the extent that all his thoughts are devoted to this subject, and he never gives any thought to things which could benefit him in this life and in the Hereafter. If he is really serious about finding a cure for this disease, then he has to follow these steps:

1. He can find out what types of food increase sexual desire, then he can reduce his intake of them, or avoid them altogether. If this does not work, then he can fast, as fasting reduces sexual desire, especially if the food eaten when he breaks his fast is moderate.

2. He should lower his gaze and avoid looking at women, as looking at women may provoke sexual desire. The Prophet ﷺ warned us, "Looking (at women) is one of the arrows of the Shaytan." Shaytan aims his arrows at the heart of man, and there is nothing to stop this arrow from reaching its target unless one lowers one's gaze. But if a person keeps looking, he is exposing his heart to these arrows, any one of which may be fatal.

3. He should enjoy permissible sex (i.e. within marriage), because any natural desire that Allah has created in us has a permissible outlet. This is the best cure, as the Prophet ﷺ has indicated.

4. He should think of the harm and damage that may befall him in this world as a consequence of his fulfilling his sexual desire in a prohibited way. Even if there were no Paradise or Hell, the harm that could be caused in this world by such an action should be enough to stop him from doing it. The damage caused by such actions is so great that it can barely be quantified, but sexual desire makes some people blind.

5. He should think of the ugliness of the person who is tempting him to commit adultery with her, especially if she is known to have other partners. He should feel too proud to drink from the same place as dogs and wolves!

Strengthening the motive of reason and religion

In the battle between reason/religion and whims/desires, we have the following "weapons" at our disposal:

1. We should remember the glory and greatness of Allah, and feel that He is too great to be sinned against as He is All-Seeing and All-Hearing. Whoever thinks of the greatness of Allah will never be at ease in committing wrong actions.

2. If we claim to love Allah, then we should not disobey Him, because of that love. A person should be obedient to the One he claims to love. Those who refrain from committing wrong action out of their love for Allah are of the highest status in His sight, as are those who worship Him out of love for Him. There is a great difference between the one who obeys Allah and abstains from wrong action out of love, and the one who does so out of fear of punishment.

3. We should think of the blessings and favours of Allah, as a decent and noble person would never act against the One who has been treating him kindly. Only base and ignoble people do such a thing. If we think of the blessings and favours of Allah, we will realise that we should not respond by going against His commands and committing wrong action.

4. We should think of the wrath and punishment of Allah, as He will be angry with the person who persists in committing wrong action. Nothing can stand in the way of the consequences of His anger, least of all this weak slave of His.

5. We should think of what the person who commits wrong action has to lose, in this world and the next. It should be sufficient to think of the loss of *iman* (faith), of which the smallest amount is worth much more than everything in this world. How can anyone be willing to lose his *iman* in return for some brief moments of pleasure, the consequences of which might last forever? In a *sahih* hadith, the Prophet ﷺ said, "No adulterer is a believer at the time when he is committing adultery." Commenting on this hadith, one of the *Sahabah* said, "His *iman* will be dragged out of him until it

goes over his head like a cloud. If he repents, then his *iman* will return to him."

6. We should relish the idea of defeating the Shaytan and being victorious over him, because overcoming him, and our whims and desires, is a thing of joy and carries a great reward. It is like taking medicine and being rewarded with restoration to good health.

7. We should bear in mind the reward and compensation which Allah has promised to those who control their whims and desires, and abstain from that which is *haram*.

8. We should think of the special companionship of Allah, as He has told us, "Allah is with those who patiently persevere" (al-Baqarah 2:153); "For Allah is with those who restrain themselves and those who do good" (an-Nahl 16:128); "For verily Allah is with those who do right." (al-'Ankabut 29:69).

9. We should be ever mindful of death, which could come upon us at any time, suddenly and without warning.

10. We should stop thinking of falsehood and bad ideas. Even if bad thoughts cross our minds, we should not let them stay, otherwise they may become hopes and wishes which we may act upon, and harm ourselves and others in the process.

11. We should gradually strengthen our religious motive in fighting whims and desires. Once we have tasted the joy of defeating those whims and desires, then our determination and willpower will grow stronger.

12. We should direct our thoughts towards contemplation of the signs of Allah which He has encouraged us to think about, whether they are in the Qur'an or in the universe around us. If such thoughts are constantly in our hearts and minds, this will help us to shun the whispering of the Shaytan. There is no greater loser than the one who, instead of thinking of Allah, His Book, His Prophet and his *Sahabah*, dwells on Shaytan and the ideas of Shaytan.

13. We should remember how short our stay on this earth is. No-one would want to feel that all he has achieved in this life is the worst

kind of deeds, except a person who has no spiritual ambition, whose heart is dead and who is careless. Such a person will ultimately regret his deeds when he realises that, far from benefiting him, they will lead to punishment. Even the person who has many good deeds to his credit will feel that sense of regret when he realises that he could have done even more.

14. We should know that Allah has created us to live an eternal life with no death, a life of pride and ease with no humiliation, a life of security with no fear, a life of richness with no poverty, a life of joy with no pain, a life of perfection with no flaws. Allah is testing us in this world with a life that will end in death, a life of pride that is accompanied by humiliation and degradation, a life that is tainted by fear, where joy and ease are mixed with sorrow and pain. So many people are mistakenly seeking an easy life of power and pleasure in this world, but most of them never manage to achieve it, and those who do, enjoy it only for a brief time before it vanishes. The Prophets called people to an eternal life of plenty, and whoever answers their call will have the best life in this world, better than the life of kings and their followers, for *zuhd* in this life is true richness. This is something for which the Shaytan greatly envies the believers.

Merely knowing the facts that we have outlined above is not enough. We have to strive and do our utmost to achieve our aim and attain perfection. The best way to do so is to put a stop to the habits that are controlling our lives, as these are the main obstacles which prevent us from succeeding. We should avoid places of *fitnah* and temptation, as the Prophet ﷺ told us, "Whoever hears of the *Dajjal* should keep away from him." The best way to protect ourselves from wrong is to keep away from anything that could lead to it. One of the favourite tricks of the Shaytan, which deceives everyone except those who are clever enough to see it, is to show a person some goodness in a wrong thing, and call him to go towards what is good; when the person gets close to it, he falls into the trap.

CHAPTER 7

Man Cannot Do Without Patience

At any given moment, a person is in a situation where he has to obey a command of Allah, or he has to stay away from something which Allah has prohibited, or he has to accept a decree of Allah, or he has to give thanks (show gratitude) for a blessing which he has received from Allah. All of these situations demand patience, so up until the time of death, no-one can do without patience. Whatever happens to us in life is either in accordance with our wishes and desires, or against them. In both cases, patience is required.

If a person enjoys good health, security, power, wealth and fulfilment of his physical desires, he should not assume that this time of ease will last forever, and he should not let his good fortune make him arrogant, extravagant or careless in a way that Allah does not like. He should not devote all his time, money and energy to the pursuit of physical pleasure, because too much pleasure results in pain. He should take care to pay what is due to Allah in the way of *zakat* and *sadaqah,* otherwise Allah might take away His blessing. He should also abstain from spending money in a *haram* way, and be careful to avoid spending it in a *makruh* way. All of this takes patience, and nobody can exercise patience at a time of ease except people of very strong faith *(as-siddiqun).*

Patience at the time of adversity is easier than at the time of ease
One of the *salaf* said: "Believers and unbelievers alike may have patience at a time of adversity, but only people of strong faith can have patience at a time of ease." Therefore Allah warned against the *fitnah* of wealth, wives and children:

"O you who believe! Let not your riches or your children divert you from the remembrance of Allah. If any act thus, the loss is their own." (al-Munafiqun 63:9)

"O you who believe! Truly, among your wives and your children are (some that are) enemies to yourselves: so beware of them!" (at-Taghabun 64:14)

The enmity referred to in these *ayat* is not that which results from hatred and conflict, but that which results from love and care, that might prevent parents from religious duties such as *hijrah*, *jihad*, seeking knowledge and giving *sadaqah*.

At-Tirmidhi narrated from Ibn Abbas that a man asked him (Ibn Abbas) about the *ayah* quoted above (at-Taghabun 64:14). Ibn Abbas told him that this *ayah* refers to some men of Makkah who embraced Islam, but when they wanted to migrate to join the Prophet ﷺ in Madinah, their wives and children prevented them from doing so. Later on, when they eventually joined the Prophet ﷺ and saw that others had already learned a great deal about Islam, they wanted to punish their wives and children. So Allah revealed this *ayah*: "O you who believe! Truly, among your wives and your children are (some that are) enemies to yourselves: so beware of them!" (at-Taghabun 64:14). At-Tirmidhi said that this report is *hasan sahih*.

The hadith, "Children are the cause of cowardliness and stinginess" reflects how much a man may be held back in his pursuit of perfection and success by his wife and children. Once, when the Prophet ﷺ was delivering a *khutbah,* he saw Hasan and Hussein walking and stumbling, so he interrupted his speech and went to pick them up, and said, "Indeed, Allah has spoken the truth when He said: '...among your wives and your children are (some that are) enemies to yourselves.' I saw these two little boys stumbling and I did not have the patience to continue my *khutbah,* so I stopped and picked them up." The Prophet ﷺ did so because of his love for children, and in this way he set an example for his *Ummah* to show mercy and kindness towards children.

The reason why it is so difficult to exercise patience at a time of ease is because we have a choice regarding how to behave. A hungry person has better patience when he has no access to food, and when food becomes available, his patience weakens. Similarly, it is easier to control one's sexual desire when no women are around.

Patience in worship

We human beings have a natural aversion to carrying out acts of worship, like *salah*, because of our inherent laziness. If a man is hardhearted and commits many wrong actions, thinking too much of physical pleasure and mixing with people who do not remember Allah, then he can hardly perform his prayers, and if he does pray he does so absent-mindedly and hurriedly.

Every step of the way, man needs patience in carrying out an act of worship. Before he starts to do it, he must make sure that his intentions are correct. He should check his sincerity, and seek to avoid showing off in performing any act of worship. Whilst he is performing any act of worship, he must try to perfect it, to keep his intention pure and his mind focused on the purpose of performing that act of worship, namely that it is to please Allah. After completing an act of worship, he must abstain from doing anything that could corrupt his worship. Allah has told us: "O you who believe! Cancel not your charity by reminders of your generosity or by injury" (al-Baqarah 2:264). He should exercise patience in refraining from admiring and feeling proud of his performance, as this is more damaging than committing many other, more visible, wrong actions. Similarly, he should always be discreet and refrain from telling others about his acts of worship.

Patience in abstaining from committing wrong actions

The best way to help oneself abstain from wrong action is to break all bad habits, and forsake all those who encourage one to commit wrong actions. Habits have a strong hold over man's behaviour, and if habit is accompanied by desires, this means that there are two soldiers of Shaytan fighting the motives of reason and religion, which cannot then withstand them.

Patience in adversity and in situations beyond man's control

Trials such as the death of a beloved one, sickness, loss of wealth, etc., fall into two types: adversity beyond one's control, and adversity caused by the actions of another human being, such as slander, beating, etc.

In facing situations that are beyond one's control, people may have any of the following reactions:
1. feeling helpless and discontented, panicking and complaining.
2. responding with patience, either for the sake of Allah or as a sign of human strength.
3. accepting and being contented with the situation. This is actually of a higher status than patience.
4. accepting the situation with thanks and gratitude. This is even higher than acceptance, because in this case a person sees the adversity as a blessing and thanks Allah for putting him through it.

Problems and adversity that befall a person at the hands of others may be faced with any of the following reactions:
1. he may choose to forgive and forget.
2. he may decide not to take revenge.
3. he may accept the decree *(qada' wa qadr)*, whilst recognising that the person who harmed him was a wrong-doer, yet the One Who decreed that this harm should reach him at the hands of the wrong-doer is not a wrong-doer. The harm caused by people is like heat and cold: there is no way to prevent it happening and the one who complains about

heat and cold betrays a lack of wisdom. Everything that happens, happens through the decree *(qada' wa qadr),* even though there are many different ways and means for it to happen.

4. he may treat well the person who mistreated him. This attitude has many advantages and benefits, which nobody can know in their entirety except Allah.

Patience in situations which are started by choice, but whose consequences get out of hand

For example, love, the start of which may be by choice but the final consequences of which are beyond a person's control. Similarly, one may expose oneself to the causes of illness and pain (for example, by smoking or taking drugs), after which it is difficult to stop the consequences, and after taking a large amount of intoxicants it is difficult to stop drunkenness. Man should exercise patience and abstain in the first place.

Chapter 8

What is the Most Difficult Type of Patience?

The degree of difficulty in abstaining from some things depends on the strength of one's motive and one's ability to do the action in question. Whoever has no motive to kill, or steal, or drink alcohol, or whatever, and at the same time is not able to do it, will find it very easy to exercise patience in abstaining from those things. Whoever has a strong motive to commit a wrong action and has the means to do so, will face great difficulty in exercising enough patience to abstain. Therefore it is very difficult for a ruler to refrain from committing injustice and oppression *(dhulm)*, and it is difficult for a young man to refrain from fornication, and it is difficult for a rich man to refrain from pursuing physical desires and pleasures.

The Prophet ﷺ is reported to have said, "Allah will commend a young man who never behaved in an ignorant way" (Ahmad). In another hadith, he referred to those who will be shaded in the shade of Allah's throne for their perfect patience – such as the patience of an absolute ruler in being just in all situations, regardless of his own feelings, and the patience of a young man in worshipping and obeying Allah and suppressing his own whims and desires, and the patience of the man who stayed in the mosque, and the patience of the man who gives *sadaqah* in keeping his *sadaqah* secret, and the patience of a man who resists the temptation of a woman of beauty and high status, and the patience of two men who meet for the sake of Allah and part for the sake of Allah, in keeping their relationship for the sake of Allah, and the patience of one who weeps out of fear of Allah, in keeping that secret and not telling others about it. All of these are among the most difficult types of patience. Therefore the punishment of an old man who commits adultery, a king who tells lies and a poor man who is arrogant is more severe, because it is easy for them to keep away from such wrong actions, and does not require much in the way of patience. Their attitude indicates that they are wilfully rebelling against Allah.

Patience in abstaining from wrong actions of speech and sexual wrong actions

Among the most difficult types of patience is patience in refraining from committing wrong actions of speech and sexual wrong actions. Wrong actions of speech - such as backbiting and slander, telling lies to create trouble between people, and praising oneself explicitly or implicitly, and insulting people one does not like and praising those whom one does like - are all entertaining and enjoyable. There is a strong motive to commit these wrong actions, and it is so easy to move one's tongue and speak, so the patience required to abstain from them is particularly difficult. Therefore the Prophet ﷺ told Mu'adh, "Control your tongue." Mu'adh asked, "Are we accountable for what we say?" The Prophet ﷺ answered, "Is there anything other than the wrong actions of speech that cause people to be thrown in Hell on their faces?"

Once the wrong actions of speech have become a habit, patience becomes even more difficult. So you might see a man who stays up all night praying, fasts all day, and would refrain from touching a pillow if it were made of silk, yet he gives his tongue free rein in backbiting, slandering and causing trouble between people.

43

CHAPTER 9

Patience in the Qur'an

Imam Ahmad said, "Allah has mentioned patience in the Qur'an in ninety places." Here, we will list the different contexts in which patience appears.

1. Instruction. Patience is enjoined upon believers:
   > *"And be patient for your patience is but by Allah..."* (an-Nahl 16:127)

   > *"Now await in patience the command of your Lord..."* (at-Tur 52:48)

2. That which is opposite to patience is forbidden:
   > *"...and be in no haste about the (Unbelievers)..."* (al-Ahqaf 46:35)

   > *"So lose not heart nor fall in despair..."* (Al 'Imran 3:139)

   > *"...and be not like the Companion of the Fish (i.e. Yunus ﷺ) - when he cried out in agony."* (al-Qalam 68:48)

3. Patience is made a condition of success and prosperity:
   > *"O you who believe! Persevere in patience and constancy; vie in such perseverance; strengthen each other; and fear Allah; that you may prosper."* (Al 'Imran 3:200)

4. The rewards of those who exercise patience will be doubled:
   > *"Twice will they be given their reward, for that they have persevered..."* (al-Qasas 28:54)

"...Those who patiently persevere will truly receive a reward without measure!" (az-Zumar 39:10)

Sulayman ibn Qasim said that the reward of every deed is known, except for the reward of patience, which will be like heavy rain.

5. Patience and *iman* are prerequisites for leadership in religion:
"And We appointed, from among them, leaders, giving guidance under Our commands, so long as they persevered with patience and continued to have faith in Our Signs." (as-Sajdah 32:24)

6. Patience is the way to earn the companionship of Allah:
"...and be patient and persevering: for Allah is with those who patiently persevere." (al-Anfal 8:46)

Abu Ali ad-Daqqaq said, "People who have patience are the true winners in this world and the next, because they have the companionship of Allah."

7. Allah will reward those who have patience with a three-fold reward - blessings, mercy and guidance:
"...but give glad tidings to those who patiently persevere - who say, when afflicted with calamity: 'To Allah we belong, and to Him is our return' - they are those on whom (descend) blessings from their Lord, and Mercy and they are the ones that receive guidance." (al-Baqarah 2:155-7)
When people came to offer their condolences to one of the *salaf*, for some calamity that had befallen him, he said, "Why should I not practice patience, when Allah has promised those who have patience three rewards, each of which is better than this world and everything in it?"

8. Patience is a means of seeking Allah's help:
"...seek (Allah's) help with patient perseverance and prayer..." (al-Baqarah 2:45)
So whoever has no patience has no help.

9. Patience and *taqwa* are conditions for Allah's help and support:
   "Yea - if you remain firm, and act aright, even if the enemy should rush here on you in hot haste, your Lord would help you with five thousand angels making a terrific onslaught." (Al 'Imran 3:125)

10. Patience and *taqwa* are a great protection against the cunning of enemies:
   "...But if you are constant and do right, not the least harm will their cunning do to you..." (Al 'Imran 3:120)

11. The angels will salute the people of patience in *Jannah*:
   "...and angels shall enter unto them from every gate (with the salutation): 'Peace unto you for that you persevered in patience! Now how excellent is the final Home!'" (ar-Ra'd 13:24)

12. Allah made it permissible to treat our enemies no worse than they treat us, but He has made it clear that practising patience is better:
   "And if you do catch them out, catch them out no worse than they catch you out: but if you show patience, that is indeed the best (course) for those who are patient." (an-Nahl 16:126)

13. Allah made patience and right actions a condition for forgiveness and great reward:
   "Not so those who show patience and constancy, and work righteousness; for them is forgiveness (of wrong actions) and a great reward." (Hud 11:11)

14. Allah has made patience a standard of courage and determination in the conduct of one's affairs:
   "But indeed if any show patience and forgive, that would truly be an exercise of courageous will and resolution in the conduct of affairs." (ash-Shura 42:43)

"(Luqman said:) 'O my son! ...enjoin what is just, and forbid what is wrong: and bear with patient constancy whate'er betide you, for this is firmness (of purpose) in (the conduct of) affairs." (Luqman 31:17)

15. Allah has promised the believers His support and victory, and has said that they deserve this because of their patience:
"...The fair promise of your Lord was fulfilled for the Children of Israel, because they had patience and constancy..." (al-A'raf 7:137)

16. Allah has made patience a condition of His love:
"How many of the Prophets fought (in Allah's way), and with them (fought) large bands of godly men? But they never lost heart if they met with disaster in Allah's way, nor did they weaken (in will) nor give in. And Allah loves those who are firm and steadfast (as-sabirin)." (Al 'Imran 3:146)

17. Allah has made patience a condition of receiving many blessings:
"But those who had been granted (true) knowledge said: 'Alas for you! The reward of Allah (in the Hereafter) is best for those who believe and work righteousness: but this none shall attain, save those who steadfastly persevere (in good).'" (al-Qasas 28:80)

"And no one will be granted such goodness except those who exercise patience and self-restraint – none but persons of the greatest good fortune." (Fussilat 41:35)

18. Allah has mentioned that only those who practise patience and gratitude will benefit from the Signs of Allah:
"Do you not see that the ships sail through the ocean by the grace of Allah? - that He may show you of His Signs? Verily in this are Signs for all who constantly persevere and give thanks." (Luqman 31:31)

"And among His Signs are the ships, smooth-running through the ocean, (tall) as mountains. If it be His Will, He can still the Wind: then they would become motionless on the back of the (ocean). Verily in this are Signs for everyone who patiently perseveres and is grateful." (ash-Shura 42:32-33)

19. Allah praised Ayyub ﷺ for his patience:
"...Truly We found him full of patience and constancy, how excellent in Our service! Ever did he turn (to Us)!" (Sad 38:44)

Allah described Ayyub ﷺ as excellent because of his patience, so the person who fails to exercise patience when it is necessary will be regarded as a failure and a sinner.

20. Allah has given a general ruling that whoever does not have faith and does not belong to the people of truth and patience, is in a state of loss. This means that the only true winners are people of patience:
"By (the Token of) Time (through the Ages), verily Man is in loss, except such as have Faith, and do right actions, and (join together) in the mutual teaching of Truth, and of Patience and Constancy." (al-'Asr 103:1-3)

Commenting on this *surah*, Imam ash-Shafi'i said, "If people thought deeply enough about this *surah*, it would provide enough guidance, as man cannot attain perfection without perfecting these two things, his knowledge and his actions, i.e. his faith and right actions. As he is required to perfect himself, so he is required to perfect others, which is joining together in mutual teaching of the truth. The foundation of all this is patience."

21. Allah has mentioned that the main characteristic of those who attain salvation is patience and compassion:

"Then will he be of those who believe and enjoin patience, (constancy, and self-restraint), and enjoin deeds of kindness and compassion. Such are the companions of the right hand." (al-Balad 90:17-18)

22. Allah has mentioned patience...

a) alongside the pillars of Islam and *iman*, as He has mentioned it alongside *salah*: *"Nay, seek (Allah's) help with patient perseverance and prayer..."* (al-Baqarah 2:45);

b) alongside right actions: *"Not so those who show patience and constancy, and do right actions; for them is forgiveness (of wrong actions) and a great reward,"* (Hud 11:11);

c) alongside gratitude *(shukr)*: *"...Verily in this are Signs for everyone who patiently perseveres and is grateful."* (ash-Shura 42:32-33);

d) alongside truth: *"...and (join together) in the mutual teaching of truth, and of patience and constancy."* (al-'Asr 103:1-3);

e) alongside compassion: *"...those who believe and enjoin patience, (constancy, and self-restraint), and enjoin deeds of kindness and compassion..."* (al-Balad 90:17);

f) alongside faith: *"...so long as they persevered with patience and continued to have faith in Our Signs."* (as-Sajdah 32:24);

g) alongside truth: *"...for true men and women, for men and women who are patient and constant..."* (al-Ahzab 33:35).

Allah has made patience the means for attaining His love, His companionship, His help and support, and His good rewards. This is sufficient honour and blessings.

CHAPTER 10
Ahadith about Patience

Umm Salamah ﷺ said: I heard the Prophet ﷺ saying, "There is no Muslim afflicted with calamity who says, 'To Allah we belong and to Him is our return; O Allah reward me for this calamity and compensate me with what is better for me,' but Allah will compensate him with what is better for him." She said, "When Abu Salamah died, I said, 'Who among Muslims is better than Abu Salamah? His household was the first to migrate to the Messenger of Allah!' Anyhow, I said what the Prophet ﷺ taught us to say, and Allah compensated me with the Messenger of Allah. The Prophet ﷺ sent Hatib ibn Abi Balta'ah to ask for my hand in marriage on his behalf, but I told him that I had a daughter, and that I was a very jealous woman. The Prophet ﷺ responded, 'As far as her daughter is concerned, I shall pray to Allah to make her independent, and I shall pray to Allah to take away her jealousy.' So I married the Messenger ﷺ." (Muslim)

Abu Musa al-Ash'ari said: The Prophet ﷺ said, "When a child of a man dies, Allah asks the angels, 'Did you take the soul of My slave's child?' They reply, 'Yes.' He asks them, 'Did you take away the apple of his eye?', and they reply, 'Yes.' Then He asks, 'What did My slave say?' They tell Him, 'He praised You and said, "To Allah we belong and to Him is our return."' Allah says, 'Build a house for him in Paradise and call it *bait al-hamd* (the house of praise).'" (At-Tirmidhi, Ahmad and Ibn Hibban)

Anas ﷺ narrated that the Prophet ﷺ said: "Allah said, 'If I test My slave by depriving him of his two precious ones (meaning his eyes or eyesight), and he faces that with patient perseverance, I shall compensate him with Paradise." (al-Bukhari)

From 'A'ishah ﷺ via 'Urwah and az-Zuhri: "The Prophet ﷺ said, 'No affliction befalls a Muslim but Allah forgives his wrong actions because of it, even if it be no more than a thorn.'" (al-Bukhari and Muslim)

Sa'd ibn Abi Waqqas ﷺ said: "I asked the Prophet ﷺ who among the people are most severely tried? He said, "The Prophets, then the right acting people, and so on down through various categories of people. Man will be tested according to the strength of his faith. The stronger his faith, the more severe his trial, and the weaker his faith, the lighter his trial. The believer will be continually tested until he walks on earth with all his wrong actions forgiven.'" (al-Bukhari)

Anas ﷺ narrated that a son of Abu Talhah ﷺ fell ill and died one day when Abu Talhah was away from home. When Abu Talhah's wife realised that her son had died, she covered him with a blanket, and left him lying by the wall. Abu Talhah came home and asked how the boy was, and his wife told him, "He has calmed down and I hope he is resting", so Abu Talhah thought that the child was getting better. That night he slept with his wife, and in the morning he got up and performed *ghusl*. When he was about to go out, his wife told him that his son had died. So Abu Talhah went and prayed with the Prophet ﷺ, then told him what had happened. The Prophet ﷺ responded by saying, "May Allah bless this last night of yours." A man from the *Ansar* said, "I have seen nine children of the man who was born as a result of that night, and all of them have read the Qur'an." (al-Bukhari)

Abu Sa'id al-Khudri ﷺ reported that the Prophet ﷺ said: "No-one can be given a better and more abundant gift than patience." (al-Bukhari and Muslim)

Patience at the time of sickness
Abu Sa'id al-Khudri ﷺ said: "I entered upon the Prophet ﷺ when he was sick and had a high temperature. I put my hand on the cover with

which he was covering himself and I could feel the heat of his fever. I said, 'How strong is your fever, O Messenger of Allah!' He said, 'We Prophets are like that: our pain is multiplied so our rewards will be multiplied.'" (Ahmad)

Jabir ibn Abdullah 🏵 said that the Messenger of Allah 🏵 entered upon a woman and asked her, "Why are you shivering like that?" She said, "It is because of fever," and cursed the fever. The Prophet 🏵 said, "Do not slander fever, because it takes away many wrong actions, just as the blacksmith's bellows remove dross and impurities from iron." (Muslim)

Ziyad ibn Ziyad, the *mawla* (freed slave) of Ibn Abbas 🏵, narrated from one of the *Sahabah*, who said: "We entered upon the Prophet 🏵 when he was ill with fever. We expressed our sorrow for his pain, and said, 'May our mothers and fathers be sacrificed for you, O Messenger of Allah! How severe is your pain!' He replied, 'We Prophets are afflicted many times more strongly.' We said, 'Subhan'Allah!' He asked, 'Do you find this strange? There were some Prophets who were killed by ringworm.' We said, 'Subhan'Allah!' He asked, 'Do you find this strange? The most severely tried of people are the Prophets, then the right acting people, then those who are less right acting, and so on.' We said, 'Subhan'Allah!' He said, 'Do you find this strange? They used to enjoy their times of trials and affliction as you enjoy your times of ease.'"

Masruq narrated from 'A'ishah 🏵 who said: "I have never seen anyone endure more severe pain than the Prophet 🏵. When he fell ill, his pain became so severe, to the extent that he could not sleep for nineteen nights."

'A'ishah 🏵 narrated that the Messenger of Allah 🏵 said: "Truly fever makes wrong actions fall away from a man like leaves fall from a tree." And it was narrated that the Prophet 🏵 said: "The likeness of the believer when he suffers from illness is like iron when it enters the fire; the dross is removed, and the good elements stay."

It was narrated that Abu Ayyub al-Ansari ﷺ said: "The Prophet ﷺ visited a sick man of the *Ansar*, and when the Prophet ﷺ asked how he was, he said, 'O Messenger of Allah, I have not closed my eyes for seven days.' The Prophet ﷺ told him, 'Have patience, my brother, for if you do, you will be rid of your wrong actions as easily as you acquired them.' The Prophet ﷺ also said, 'The time of illness cancels out the time of wrong actions.'"

Anas ﷺ narrated that the Prophet ﷺ said: "When a slave of Allah becomes ill for three days, he will come out having shed all his wrong actions, and will become as sinless as the day he was born." And it was narrated that the Prophet ﷺ said, "The prayer of the sick person will never be rejected, until he recovers."

It was narrated that the Prophet ﷺ said: "By the One in Whose hand is my soul, there is no *qada'* that Allah decrees for the believer but it is good for him. If Allah decrees that he will go through a time of ease, the believer will be grateful, and that is good for him. If Allah decrees that he will suffer some affliction, he will be patient, and that is also good for him. This applies only to believers." (Ahmad)

CHAPTER 11

Sahabah on the Virtues of Patience

As-Safar said: Abu Bakr fell ill, so some people visited him and asked whether they should call a doctor for him. He said, "The Doctor has already seen me." They asked, "What did he say?" Abu Bakr said, "He said, 'I do what I want.'" (Meaning, that Allah is his "Doctor" and can make him sick or healthy as He wills). (Ahmad)

'Umar ibn al-Khattab ؓ said, "The best days we ever lived were by virtue of patience, and if patience were to take the shape of a man, he would be a noble and generous man."

Ali ibn Abi Talib ؓ said, "The relation of patience to *iman* is like the relation of the head to the body. If the head is chopped off, the body becomes useless." Then he raised his voice and said, "Certainly, the one who has no patience has no *iman,* and patience is like a riding-beast that never gets tired."

'Umar ibn 'Abdul-'Aziz said, "Allah never bestows a blessing on His slave then takes it away and compensates him by giving him patience, but that with which he has been compensated is better than that which has been taken away from him."

The story of 'Urwah ibn al-Zubayr
'Urwah ibn al-Zubayr came to visit the Khalifah al-Walid ibn 'Abdul-Malik. With him was his son Muhammad, who was one of the most handsome of men. The young man had dressed up for the occasion in fine clothes, and had his hair in two plaits or braids. When al-Walid saw him, he said, "This is how the young people of Quraysh should look!" and by so saying, put the evil eye on him. Before he left, the young man

fell ill. When he was in the stable (preparing for the journey) he fell down, and the horses trampled him to death.

Then 'Urwah got gangrene in his leg, and al-Walid sent doctors to him, who suggested that the leg should be amputated, otherwise the gangrene would spread to the rest of his body and kill him. 'Urwah agreed, and the doctors began to remove his leg, using a saw. When the saw reached the bone, 'Urwah fainted, and when he came around, sweat was pouring down his face, and he was repeating, "La ilaha ill-Allah, Allahu akbar". When the operation was over, he picked up his leg and kissed it, then said, "I swear by the One Who mounted me on you, I never used you to walk to any place of wrong action or to any place where Allah would not like me to be." Then he gave instructions that the leg should be washed, perfumed, wrapped in a cloth and buried in the Muslim graveyard.

When 'Urwah left al-Walid and returned to Madinah, his family and friends went to meet him at the outskirts of the city and to offer their condolences. The only reply he made was to quote from the Qur'an: "...truly we have suffered much fatigue at our journey" (al-Kahf 18:62). He did not say any more than that. Then he said, "I will not enter Madinah, for people there either rejoice over the afflictions of others, or else feel envy for their blessings." So he went to stay in a palace at al-'Aqiq. 'Isa ibn Talhah came to visit him there and said, "May your enemies' fathers perish!" and asked him, "Show me the affliction for which I have come to console you." 'Urwah uncovered his stump, and 'Isa said, "By Allah, we were not preparing you to wrestle! Allah has saved most of you: your sanity, your tongue, your eyesight, your two hands, and one of your two legs." 'Urwah told him, "Nobody has consoled me as you have."

When the doctors came to perform the amputation, they had asked 'Urwah whether he would drink intoxicants to ease the pain. He said,

"Allah is testing me to see the extent of my patience. How could I go against His commands?"

Beautiful patience (sabr jamil – Surah Yusuf 12:83) and panic
Mujahid said, "Beautiful patience is patience without any panic." Amr ibn Qays said, "Beautiful patience means to be content with adversity and to surrender to the will of Allah."

Yunus ibn Yazid said: I asked Rabi'ah ibn 'Abdul-Rahman, "What is the ultimate of patience?" He said, "To be outwardly the same at the time of affliction as one was the day before it struck." (This does not mean that a person does not or should not feel pain or anguish; patience in this instance means that one refrains from panicking and complaining.)

Commenting on the meaning of beautiful patience, Qiyas ibn al-Hajjaj said, "The person who is suffering from some affliction should behave in such a way that nobody is able to distinguish him from others."

CHAPTER 12

Patience at the Time of Bereavement

The loss of a loved one is a time when a person may be overwhelmed with grief, and many customs surrounding bereavement reflect the depth of the feeling of loss. Wailing, eulogizing (i.e. praising the deceased excessively) and tearing one's garments are all customs which were known at the time of *Jahiliyyah*, and are still common among some Muslims. Such conduct is not permitted in Islam, as the believer is required to face bereavement, like all other trials of life, with patience.

It is permitted to cry or weep, softly, before death, at the time of death, and after the person has died. According to ash-Shafi'i, however, it is *makruh* to cry after the person has died, but permissible before the soul has departed.

The correct opinion is that crying is permitted both before and after death. The evidence for this is the hadith narrated by Jabir ibn 'Abdullah ﷺ in which he said, "My father died at the battle of Uhud, and I began to weep. The people told me to stop, but the Messenger of Allah ﷺ never asked me to stop. Then my aunt Fatimah began to weep too, and the Prophet ﷺ said, 'It does not matter whether you cry or not, the angels kept shading him until they ascended with his soul.'" (Agreed upon)

Ibn 'Abbas ﷺ reported that when Ruqayyah ﷺ, the daughter of the Prophet ﷺ, died, the women started to cry, and 'Umar ﷺ began to whip them to make them stop. The Prophet ﷺ told him, "O 'Umar, leave them alone and let them cry." To the women he said, "Go ahead and cry, but avoid the crying of the Shaytan... Whatever comes from your eye and heart is from Allah and is a sign of mercy, and whatever comes from your hand and your tongue is from the Shaytan." (Ahmad)

A number of sound *ahadith* describe the Prophet ﷺ weeping on a number of occasions when someone he loved had died. When the Prophet ﷺ visited the tomb of his mother he wept, and caused others to weep. When he was burying the martyr 'Uthman ibn Madh'un ﷺ after Uhud, he kissed him and his tears fell on 'Uthman's face. When he gave the news of the death of Ja'far ﷺ and his companions in the battle against the Romans at Mu'tah, he spoke with tears streaming down his face. Another sound report describes how Abu Bakr ﷺ wept when he kissed the Prophet ﷺ after he had died. The *ahadith* that forbid crying should be interpreted as referring to the kind of crying that is accompanied by eulogizing and wailing.

Eulogizing and wailing

Eulogizing the dead and wailing in grief are *haram*, according to Ahmad, ash-Shafi'i and others. In a hadith narrated from Abdullah ibn Mas'ud ﷺ, the Prophet ﷺ said, "He is not one of us who strikes himself on the cheeks, rends his garment and behaves like the people of *Jahiliyyah*." (al-Bukhari and Muslim)

Umm 'Atiyyah ﷺ said, "When we gave our allegiance to him, the Prophet ﷺ asked us never to wail (at the time of bereavement)." (al-Bukhari and Muslim)

Abu Malik al-Ash'ari ﷺ said: "The Prophet ﷺ said, 'There are four habits which my *Ummah* has, which are from the *Jahiliyyah*. My *Ummah* will never rid itself of them. They are: seeking pride in noble descent; slandering one another by casting doubts on one another's lineage; seeking rain through astrology; and wailing.'" In another hadith, the Prophet ﷺ said that if a woman practices the custom of wailing, and does not repent before she dies, on the Day of Resurrection she will be raised with clothes of tar and a shield of scabs. (Muslim)

Abu Musa ﷺ said: The Prophet ﷺ said, "The deceased person suffers because of the wailing of the living. When the wailing woman says, 'What a great loss! I have lost my right arm, the one who clothed me', the deceased will be pulled up sharply and asked, 'Are you her right hand? Are you her support? Are you the one who clothed her?'" (Ahmad)

There is no doubt that wailing and eulogizing are *haram*. How could it be otherwise, when they indicate discontent with one's Lord and contradict patience? Behaving this way harms oneself too, when one slaps one's face, pulls out one's own hair, prays to Allah to take one's soul, wastes possessions by tearing one's own clothes, complains of injustice from Allah and praises the deceased with qualities that he did not possess. Any one of these would be sufficient grounds for the total prohibition of wailing and eulogizing.

Saying a few words

It is permissible to say a few words when crying over a deceased person, so long as these words are true, and are not accompanied by wailing or expressions of discontent with the decree of Allah. Such brief words do not contradict patience, and are not *haram*. Anas ﷺ reported that Abu Bakr ﷺ entered upon the Prophet ﷺ after he had passed away, put his hands on his temples, kissed him between the eyes and said, "O my Prophet, O my dearest friend, O my beloved." (Ahmad)

Anas ﷺ reported that when the Prophet ﷺ became very ill, he started to lose consciousness. Fatimah ﷺ said, "How great is the distress of my father!" He said, "There will be no more distress for your father after today." When the Prophet ﷺ passed away, she said, "O my father who answered the call of his Lord, O my father whose destination is Paradise, O my father, to Jibril will tell the news of your death." After the Prophet ﷺ had been buried, she said, "O Anas, how could you bear to bury the Prophet and cover him with dust?" (al-Bukhari)

When his son Ibrahim died, the Prophet ﷺ said, "We are very sad for your death, O Ibrahim." This does not indicate discontent with the decree of Allah or complaining against Allah. Such statements are no more than crying or weeping.

The deceased person suffers because of people's wailing for him

A *sahih* hadith narrated from 'Umar ibn al-Khattab ﷺ and his son, and al-Mughirah ibn Shu'bah ﷺ indicates that a deceased person suffers because of people's wailing over him. There should be no problem in understanding this hadith, and it should not be seen as contradicting the Qur'an or the basic principles of Shari'ah. It does not mean that a man can be punished because of another person's deeds. The Prophet ﷺ did not say that the deceased person will be punished because of his family's crying over him. What he said was that the deceased suffers because of that, meaning that it hurts him. Similarly, a dead person in the grave might suffer when a person in a neighbouring grave is being punished, just as in this life it hurts him to see his neighbour being punished. So when the family of a deceased person cries, wails and eulogizes him, like the people of *Jahiliyyah* used to do, the deceased person will be hurt in his grave because of it. This is the suffering that is referred to in the hadith.

CHAPTER 13

Patience is Half of Iman

Iman is in two halves: half is patience *(sabr)* and half is gratitude *(shukr)*. Therefore Allah has mentioned patience and gratitude alongside one another:

"...*Verily in this are signs for all who constantly persevere and give thanks.*" (Ibrahim 14:5; Luqman 31:31; Saba' 34:19; ash-Shura 42:33)

The reasons why one half of *iman* is patience and the other half is gratitude are as follows:

1. *Iman* is a term which covers words, deeds and intentions, all of which are based on one of two things, action or abstinence. Action refers to performing a deed in accordance with the instructions of Allah, which is the reality of gratitude. Abstinence, as in refraining from wrong action, requires patience. The whole of religion is embodied in these two things: carrying out that which Allah has commanded, and refraining from that which Allah has prohibited.

2. Iman is based on two pillars: *yaqin* (conviction) and patience, which are referred to in the following *ayah*:

"*And We appointed, from among them, leaders, giving guidance under Our command, so long as they persevered with patience and continued to have faith in Our Signs.*" (as-Sajdah 32:24)

It is through faith that we know the reality of Allah's commands and prohibitions, of reward and punishment, and it is through patience that we carry out His instructions and abstain from that which He has prohibited. A person can never come to believe in Allah's commands and prohibitions, and in reward and punishment, except through faith, and that is truly from Allah. And we can never carry out Allah's instructions and abstain from that which He has prohibited except through patience. Therefore patience is half of *iman*, and the other half is gratitude.

3. Man has two powers, the power of doing and the power of abstaining, which control all his behaviour. So a person will do what he likes and abstain from what he dislikes. The whole of religion is doing or abstaining, carrying out the instructions of Allah or abstaining from that which He has prohibited, neither of which can be accomplished without patience.

4. The whole of religion is hope and fear, and the true believer is the one who is both hopeful and fearful. Allah says:

> *"They used to call on Us with love and reverence, and humble themselves before Us."* (al-Anbiya 21:90)

The Prophet ﷺ used to pray: "O Allah, I have surrendered my soul to You, and turned my face to You. My (own) affair I commit to Allah and I seek Your protection, in hope of You and in fear of You" (al-Bukhari). So the believer is the one who is both hopeful and fearful, but hope and fear can only be based on the foundation of patience: fear should make the believer patient, and his hope should lead to gratitude.

5. Any action done by man is either beneficial or harmful to him in this world and the next, or else it is beneficial to him in one world and harmful to him in the other. The best course for man is to do that which is beneficial to him in the Hereafter, and abstain from that which is harmful to him in the Hereafter. This is the reality of *iman*: to do what is good for him, and that is gratitude; and to abstain from that which harms him, and that is patience.

6. Man is always in a situation where he has to carry out an instruction from Allah, or avoid something which Allah has prohibited, or accept

something that Allah has decreed. In all cases, he has to face the situation with patience and gratitude. Carrying out Allah's instructions is gratitude, and abstaining from prohibited things and being content with the decree of Allah constitutes patience.

7. Man is constantly being pulled in two opposing directions: should he respond to the lure of this world of desires and pleasures, or should he answer the call of Allah and the Hereafter, with the eternal Paradise that Allah has prepared for His friend *(wali)*? Going against the call of whims and desires is patience, and responding to the call of Allah and the Hereafter is gratitude.

8. Religion is based on two principles: determination and perseverance (patience), which are referred to in the *du'a* of the Prophet ﷺ: "O Allah, I ask You for perseverance in all my affairs, and I ask You for the determination to stay on the straight and narrow path."

9. Religion is based on truth *(haqq)* and patience, which is referred to in the *ayah*:
"*...and they (join together) in the mutual teaching of truth, and of patience and constancy.*" (al-'Asr 103:3)

Man is required to work according to the truth, both by himself and with others, which is the reality of gratitude, but he cannot do that without patience, therefore patience is half of *iman*. And Allah knows best.

CHAPTER 14

Patience and Loving Allah

Patience is one of the most important qualities demanded of those who claim to love Allah, as the degree of patience determines those who are sincere in their claim and those who are not. The degree of patience needed to endure hardship and difficulties in order to please the Beloved proves the sincerity of one's love. Many claim to love Allah, but when Allah tests them with hardship, they forget the true essence of love. No-one can adhere to the love of Allah except those who are patient and persevering *(as-sabirun)*. If it were not for the test of hardship and sincerity, there would be no proof of the sincerity of a person's love for Allah. The one whose love of Allah is greater, has a greater degree of patience.

Therefore, Allah has attributed the quality of patience to His close friends *(awliya')* and most beloved. He said about His beloved slave Ayyub ﷺ: "...Truly We found him full of patience and constancy. How excellent in Our service! Ever did he turn (to Us)!" (Sad 38:44). Allah instructed the most beloved to Him of everything He created to have patience in accepting His decree and told him that patience comes only by the help of Allah. He praised those who have patience and promised them the best of rewards: the rewards of others are defined and limited, but the reward *of as-sabirun* is without measure. Patience is vital at all levels of Islam, *iman* and *ihsan*, as well as being a major element in *iman* (faith) and *tawakkul* (putting one's trust in Allah).

Patience for the sake of Allah, by the help of Allah, and in accepting the decree of Allah
1. Patience for the sake of Allah, hoping for His rewards and fearing His punishment.

2. Patience by the help of Allah, as man realises that he has no patience himself, and has no power to acquire patience. Rather, he knows: "There is no power and no strength except by (the help of) Allah."

3. Patience in accepting the decree of Allah, as man realises that Allah is the only One Who is controlling the affairs of the universe, so he will patiently accept the ruling and decree of Allah, regardless of what it may mean for him in the way of ease or hardship.

Patience for the sake of Allah is of a higher degree than patience by the help of Allah, as patience for the sake of Allah is related to His being *ilah* (god, object of worship), whilst patience by His help is related to His being *rabb* (Lord, Cherisher and Sustainer). Whatever is connected to His being *ilah,* such as patience for His sake, is worship, and as such is greater than whatever is connected to His being *rabb,* such as seeking His help in having patience. Worship is the ultimate goal, whereas seeking help is a means to that end. The goal is sought for its own sake, but means are sought for the sake of other things. Patience by His help is common to believers and unbelievers, good and bad, alike, while patience for His sake is the way of Messengers, Prophets and true believers. Patience for His sake is patience in matters that please Allah, while patience by His help may apply to matters that please Him or displease Him.

Patience in obeying Allah's commands and abstaining from that which He has prohibited is greater than patience in accepting the decree of Allah, because the patience involved in obedience comes by choice, but the patience involved in accepting His decrees is forced upon a person.

Different degrees of patience
1. Patience both for the sake of Allah and by the help of Allah. A person will have patience by the help of Allah for the sake of Allah, realising that he has no power of his own whatsoever. This is the highest degree of patience.

2. Patience for the sake of Allah but not by the help of Allah. Such people may want to have patience for the sake of Allah, but they are not actively seeking His help, and their trust and reliance *(tawakkul)* is weak. Such people will have a good ending, but they are weak and cannot achieve most of what they want to achieve. This is the situation of a sincere but weak believer.

3. Patience by the help of Allah. Such a person seeks Allah's help and puts his trust in Him, admitting that he has no power or strength whatsoever, but his patience is not for the sake of Allah, as his patience is not for reasons of faith. This will achieve his aims, but his ending may be the worst. An example of such people are the leaders of the *kuffar* and the followers of the Shaytan, as their patience is by the help of Allah, but is not for the sake of Allah.

4. No kind of patience whatsoever. This is the lowest degree, and a person of this type deserves all sorts of failures.

Those who have patience for the sake of Allah and by the help of Allah are those who are strong and achieve much. Those who have patience for the sake of Allah, but not by the help of Allah, are good people, but weak and helpless. Those who have patience by the help of Allah, but not for the sake of Allah, are capable, but evil. Those who have neither patience for the sake of Allah nor by the help of Allah are doomed to failure.

CHAPTER 15

Gratitude in the Qur'an

Allah tells us:

> "Then remember Me; I will remember you. Be grateful to Me, and do not reject Me." (al-Baqarah 2:152)

And He has told us that only those who are grateful to Him truly worship Him:

> "...and be grateful to Allah, if it is Him you worship."
> (al-Baqarah 2:172)

Allah has mentioned gratitude alongside *iman*, and has made it clear that He gains nothing from punishing His people if they give thanks to Him and believe in Him:

> "What can Allah gain by your punishment, if you are grateful and you believe?..." (an-Nisa 4:147)

In other words: if you carry out the duties for which you were created, namely gratitude and *iman*, why should Allah punish you?

Allah has divided people into two categories, the people of gratitude *(shukr)* and the people of ingratitude *(kufr)*. The thing most disliked by Him is *kufr* and the people of *kufr*; the thing most liked by Him is gratitude and the people of gratitude: "We showed him (i.e. man) the way: whether he be grateful or ungrateful (rests on his will)" (al-Insan 76:3).

According to the Qur'an, the Prophet Sulayman ﷺ said:

> "...This is by the grace of my Lord! - to test me whether I am grateful or ungrateful! And if any is grateful, truly his gratitude is (a gain) for

his own soul; but if any is ungrateful, truly my Lord is free of all needs, Supreme in honour!" (an-Naml 27:40)

And Allah said:

"And remember! Your Lord caused to be declared (publicly): 'If you are grateful, I will add more (favours) unto you; but if you show ingratitude, truly My punishment is terrible indeed.'" (Ibrahim 14:7)

"If you reject (Allah), truly Allah has no need of you; but He likes not ingratitude from His slaves: if you are grateful, He is pleased with you." (az-Zumar 39:7)

There are many *ayat* in the Qur'an where Allah makes a contrast between gratitude *(shukr)* and ingratitude *(kufr)*. For example:

"Muhammad is no more than a Messenger: many were the Messengers that passed away before him. If he died or were slain, will you then turn back on your heels? If any did turn back on his heels, not the least harm will he do to Allah, but Allah (on the other hand) will swiftly reward those who (serve Him) with gratitude." (Al 'Imran 3:144)

The rewards of gratitude

The reward of gratitude is unlimited:

"...If you are grateful, I will add more (favours) unto you..." (Ibrahim 14:7)

In contrast, other rewards and divine favours are conditional upon His will, for example...

• relief from poverty:

"...but if you fear poverty, soon will Allah enrich you, if He wills..." (at-Tawbah 9:28)

• answering prayers:

"Nay - on Him would you call, and if it be His Will, He would

68

remove (the distress) which occasioned your call upon Him..."
(al-An'am 6:41)

• *rizq* (sustenance, provision):
"...He gives Sustenance to whom He pleases." (ash-Shura 42:19)

• forgiveness:
"...He forgives whom He wills, and He punishes whom He wills..."
(al-Fath 48:14)

• Divine mercy:
"Again will Allah, after this, turn (in mercy) to whom He will..."
(at-Tawbah 9:27)

But Allah has made the reward for gratitude free from any conditions,
as in:
"...And swiftly shall We reward those that (serve Us with) gratitude"
(Al 'Imran 3:145)

"But Allah will swiftly reward those who (serve Him) with gratitude."
(Al 'Imran 3:144)

Iblis and gratitude

When the enemy of Allah realised the virtue of gratitude, he made his
main aim to keep people away from it:
"'Then will I assault them from before them and behind them, from
their right and their left: nor will You find, in most of them, gratitude
(for Your mercies).'" (al-A'raf 7:17)

Allah has described the people of gratitude as being very few:
"...But few of My slaves are grateful!" (Saba 43:13)

Gratitude and 'ibadah

Allah explains in the Qur'an that the only people who truly worship Him are those who give thanks (gratitude) to Him, so those who are not among the people of gratitude are not among the people of *'ibadah*:

> "...*and be grateful to Allah, if it is Him you worship.*"
> (al-Baqarah 2:172)

He instructed His slave Musa ﷺ to accept what He had bestowed upon him with gratitude:

> "...*'O Musa! I have chosen you above (other) men, by the mission I (have given you) and the words I (have spoken to you): take then the (revelation) which I give you, and be of those who give thanks.'*"
> (al-A'raf 7:144)

Allah has told us that His pleasure may be attained through gratitude:

> "...*If you are grateful, He is pleased with you...*" (az-Zumar 39:7)

Allah praised Ibrahim ﷺ for being grateful for His favours:

> "*Ibrahim was indeed a model. Devoutly obedient to Allah, (and) true in faith, and he joined not gods with Allah. He showed his gratitude for the favours of Allah, Who chose him, and guided him to a straight way.*" (an-Nahl 16:120-121)

Allah mentioned that gratitude is the purpose of creation:

> "*It is He Who brought you forth from the wombs of your mothers when you knew nothing; and He gave you hearing and sight and intelligence and affection: that you may give thanks (to Allah).*"
> (an-Nahl 16:78)

> "*Allah had helped you at Badr, when you were a contemptible little force; then fear Allah; thus may you show your gratitude.*"
> (Al 'Imran 3:123)

As well as being the purpose of creation, gratitude was also the purpose of sending the Prophet ﷺ:

"Then remember Me; I will remember you. Be grateful to Me, and do not reject Me." (al-Baqarah 2:152)

CHAPTER 16

Ahadith on Gratitude

It was reported that the Prophet ﷺ stayed up all night, standing until his feet became swollen. When he was asked, "Why are you doing this, when Allah has forgiven all your past and future wrong actions?" He replied, "Should I not be a grateful slave?" (al-Bukhari and Muslim)

The Prophet ﷺ told Mu'adh ؓ: "By Allah, I love you, so do not forget to say at the end of every *salah*, 'O Allah, help me to remember You and to give thanks to You and to worship You well.'" (Ahmad and at-Tirmidhi)

Hisham ibn 'Urwah said: "Among the *du'a* of the Prophet ﷺ is: 'O Allah, help me to remember You, to give thanks to You and to worship You well.'"

Ibn 'Abbas ؓ narrated that the Prophet ﷺ said: "There are four qualities, whoever is given them has truly been given the best in this world and the next. They are: a grateful heart (that is thankful to Allah), a remembering tongue (that mentions Allah often), an enduring body (to persevere through the trials which Allah may send), and a faithful wife (who does not cheat him of her body or his wealth)." Al-Qasim ibn Muhammad reported from 'A'ishah ؓ that the Prophet ﷺ said, "No blessing is bestowed on a slave and he realises that it is from Allah, but the reward of giving gratitude for it is written for him. Never does Allah know the regret of His slave for a wrong action he has committed, but Allah forgives his wrong action before the slave seeks forgiveness. No man buys a garment with his own money then puts it on and thanks Allah, but Allah will have forgiven him all his wrong action before the garment reaches his knees."

The Prophet ﷺ said, "Allah is pleased with His slave if, when he eats something, he thanks Allah for it, and when he drinks something, he thanks Allah for it." (Muslim)

Shu'bah said: "Al-Fadl ibn Fudalah narrated that Abu Rajah al-'Utaridi said, 'Once we saw 'Imran ibn al-Husayn wearing beautiful clothes that we have never seen before or since. 'Imran told us that the Prophet ﷺ said, "If Allah bestows His blessing on His slave, He likes to see the effect of that blessing on him."'"

Ibn Shu'aib narrated from his father and grandfather that the Prophet ﷺ said, "Eat, drink, and give sadaqah without being extravagant or showing off, as Allah likes to see the effect of His blessing on His slave."

Shu'bah narrated from Abu Ishaq from Abu'l-Akhwas who narrated that his father said: "I came to the Messenger of Allah ﷺ looking dishevelled and scruffy. He asked me, 'Do you have any possessions?' I said, 'Yes.' He asked me what sort, and I told him, 'I have all sorts. Allah has given me camels, horses, slaves and sheep.' The Prophet ﷺ said, 'If Allah has given you all of that, then let Him see His blessing on you.'"

Abu'd-Dunya narrated the hadith of Abu Abdur-Rahman as-Silmi from ash-Sha'bi, from an-Nu'man ibn Bashir, who said: "The Messenger of Allah ﷺ said, 'Speaking of Allah's blessing is gratitude and ignoring it is ingratitude (kufr). The one who does not give thanks for a small blessing will not give thanks for a great blessing, and the one who does not give thanks to people will not give thanks to Allah. To be with a group is a blessing, and to be alone is a punishment.'"

Ibn Abi'd-Dunya narrated that 'A'ishah ﷺ said that the Prophet ﷺ entered upon her one day and saw a small piece of bread on the floor, so he picked it up and wiped it, then told her, "O 'A'ishah, treat the blessing of Allah with respect, for when it departs from a household it may never come back to them."

Ad-Darwardi narrated from Amr ibn Abi Amr from Said al-Maqburi from Abu Hurairah ﷺ that the Messenger of Allah ﷺ said, "Allah said: 'The position of the believer in relation to Me is of the best: he praises Me even when I am pulling the soul from his body.'"

Abu Hurairah ﷺ narrated that the Prophet ﷺ said: "If any of you would like to see the great blessing of Allah on him, then let him look at those who are less fortunate than him, not those who appear better off than him."

CHAPTER 17

The Sahabah and Tabi'in on Gratitude

Salman al-Farsi ﷺ said, "There was a man who was given many of the luxuries of this world, and then they were taken away from him. But he continued to praise and thank Allah until everything had been taken from him, even his bed. And then he still praised and thanked Allah. Another man, who had also been given many of the luxuries of this world asked him, 'What are you praising and thanking Allah for?' The man said, 'I am praising and thanking Him for blessings which, if others asked me to give them to them in return for all that they have, I would never give them up.' 'What can they be?' asked the second man. 'Can't you see?' asked the first man. 'I have my eyesight, my tongue, my hands, my feet...'"

Mukhallad ibn al-Husayn said: "The definition of gratitude is abstaining from wrong action." Abu Hazim said: "Every blessing that does not bring you closer to Allah is a disaster." Sulayman said: "Remembering His blessings makes one love Allah."

Hammad ibn Ziyad narrated that Layth ibn Abi Burdah said: "I went to Madinah, where I met Abdullah ibn Salam, who said to me, 'Would you like to visit a place visited by the Prophet ﷺ, and we will offer you *sawiq* and dates?...' Then he said, 'When Allah gathers people on the Day of Judgement, He will remind them of His blessings. One of His slaves will say, "Remind me of something," and Allah will say, "Remember when you faced such-and-such adversity, and you prayed to Me, so I relieved you of it. Remember when you were travelling in such-and-such a place, and you asked Me to give you a travelling-companion, and I did so. Remember when you asked for the hand of so-and-so, the daughter of so-and-so, and others also asked for her hand, so I gave her to you to marry, and kept the others away." His slave will be standing before his Lord, Who will remind him of His many blessings.'" Then the narrator of this story (Layth) wept and said, "I hope that no-one will stand before his Lord in this way, because the one who does so will be punished." (i.e. if Allah has to point out that which should be obvious, this is a sign of a person's ingratitude, and he will be punished.)

Bakr ibn Abdullah al-Muzani said: "When a man faces affliction, he may pray to Allah and Allah may deliver him from adversity. Then Shaytan comes to the man and whispers, 'It was not as bad as you thought.' Thus the man's gratitude will be weakened." Zazan said: "The right of Allah over the man who is enjoying His blessings is that such a man should not use His blessings in order to commit wrong actions." A man of knowledge said: "The blessing of Allah to us in keeping the luxuries of this world away from us is greater than the blessing of that which he has given us, because Allah did not like His Prophet to have the luxuries of this world. So I prefer to live in the manner which Allah preferred for His Prophet than to live a life which He disliked for him."

Ibn Abi'd-Dunya said: "It was narrated to me that some scholars said: 'The scholar should praise Allah for having deprived him of the luxuries of this life, in the same way that he should praise Him for what He has bestowed upon him. How can you compare the blessings and luxuries for which he will be accountable to the deprivation of luxuries which is a relief from being tested, and which keeps his mind free to worship and remember Allah? So he should give thanks to Allah for all of that.'"

It has been said: "Gratitude is giving up wrong action." Ibn al-Mubarak said: "Sufyan said, 'He does not understand religion properly who does not count affliction as a blessing and ease as a disaster.'"

Gratitude of different faculties

A man said to Abu Hazim, "What is the gratitude of the eyes?" He said, "If you see good things, you speak about them, and if you see bad things, you keep quiet about it." He asked, "What is the gratitude of the ears?" He said, "If you hear something good, you accept it, and if you hear something bad, you reject it." Then he asked, "What is the gratitude of the hands?" He said, "Do not take what which does not belong to you, and do not hold back from paying the dues of Allah *(zakat)*." Then he asked, "What is the gratitude of the head?" He said, "To have knowledge in it." Then he asked, "What is the gratitude of one's private parts?" He quoted: "'Who guard their private parts, except from those joined to them in the marriage bond, or (the captives) whom their right hands possess – for (in their case) they are free from blame, but those whose desires exceed those limits are transgressors'" (al-Mu'minun 23:5-7).

As for those who only pay lip-service to gratitude, and do not give thanks with the rest of their faculties, they are like a man who has a garment and all he does with it is touch it, but he does not put it on: it will never protect him from heat, cold, snow or rain.

Prostration of gratitude

When the Messenger of Allah ﷺ used to receive good news, he would prostrate himself *(sujud)* and give thanks to Allah. 'Abdur-Rahman ibn Awf ﷺ narrated: "The Prophet ﷺ entered upon us in the mosque, stood facing the *qiblah*, then prostrated himself and remained in *sujud* for a long time. I said to him: 'O Messenger of Allah, you prostrated yourself for such a long time that we thought Allah had taken your soul.' He said, 'Jibril came to me with good news. He told me, "Allah says, 'Whoever sends blessings on you, I will send sixty blessings on him in return, and whoever salutes you, I will salute him in return,'" so I prostrated myself and gave thanks to Allah." (Ahmad)

Said ibn Mansur narrated that Abu Bakr ﷺ prostrated himself when he heard the news that Musaylimah had been killed, and Ka'b ibn Malik ﷺ prostrated himself when the Prophet ﷺ told him the good news that Allah had forgiven him.

All the good deeds of man cannot pay for one blessing of Allah

A worshipper worshipped Allah for fifty years, so Allah told him that He had forgiven him. The man said, "O Allah, what is there to forgive when I have not committed a wrong action?" So Allah caused a nerve in his neck to give him pain, so he could not sleep or pray. When the pain eased and he was able to sleep, an angel came to him, so he complained to the angel of the pain he had suffered. The angel told him, "Your Lord says to you that your fifty years of worship is to pay for the soothing of your pain."

Ibn Abi'd-Dunya mentioned that Dawud ﷺ asked Allah, "What is the least of Your blessings?" Allah revealed to him, "O Dawud, take a breath." Dawud did so, and Allah told him, "This is the least of My blessings on you."

From this we may understand the meaning of the hadith which was narrated by Ziyad ibn Thabit and Ibn Abbas ﷺ: "If Allah was to punish the people of heaven and earth, He would have done that without being unjust towards them, and if He were to have mercy on them, His Mercy would be far better for them than their deeds." (Abu Dawud)

In a *sahih* hadith the Messenger of Allah ﷺ said: "No-one will attain salvation by virtue of his deeds." The people asked, "Not even you, O Messenger of Allah?" He said, "Not even me, unless Allah covers me with His mercy and blessings." The deeds of a man cannot pay for even one of the many blessings of Allah, because even the smallest of Allah's blessings and favours far outweigh the deeds of man. So we must always bear in mind the rights which Allah has over us.

Translator's Afterword

We are living in a time of great confusion, a time where Muslims are only just beginning to rediscover their identity after centuries of decline and subjugation to others. Indeed, we are still dazzled by the achievements of others, and it is a constant struggle to reassert our Islam in the face of overwhelming pressure from Western media and technology.

Human knowledge may have advanced in leaps and bounds over the past few decades (and let us not forget that the scientific and medical progress of the West is built on a foundation laid down by Muslims!), but it is clear that people are thirsting for more than technology alone can offer. This is evident in the spread of "new-age" movements and cults, and also in the phenomenon of "self-improvement" and "personal-development" books, sales of which have mushroomed in recent years.

Such "motivational" books - and the tapes and courses that are also available - are well-presented and appear very attractive. Muslims, too, may be avid consumers of such material. But this material, which is overwhelmingly Western in orientation, only serves to further confuse the Muslim, who is already suffering from the identity crisis that has blighted followers of Islam for far too long. No doubt Islam has also the answers, so why can we not find information on "self-improvement" in Islamic texts?

In fact, when we familiarise ourselves with our Islamic heritage *(turath)*, we will find that our forebears had a great deal to say about the human condition. They examined the universe, and human beings, in the light of the Qur'an and Sunnah, and wrote much that is still pertinent to everyday life so many centuries later. The problem for English-speaking

Muslims is that, if they cannot read Arabic, this wealth of knowledge is inaccessible to them. Fortunately, however, many individuals and organisations are now making the effort to translate important books into English, so as to make the treasures of our heritage available beyond the Arabic-speaking world.

One of the most vital qualities for any person to attain is that which is known in Arabic as *sabr,* patience or perseverance. Anyone who wishes to be a better student, a more successful businessman, a wiser parent, needs patience. Similarly, anyone who wishes to fulfil his duties towards Allah, to observe all the prayers and fasts required by Islam, to treat other people well and to overcome his own shortcomings and failings *(jihadan-nafs),* also needs patience. Patience and gratitude are the keys to success in this world and the next, as we have learnt from reading the words of Ibn Qayyim al-Jawziyyah.

May Allah guide us to His Way and help us to be among *as-Sabirin* and *ash-Shakirin.*

Glossary of Terms

awliya'	see *wali*.
ayah (pl. *ayat*)	literally, "sign" or "miracle"; a "verse" of the Qur'an.
Dajjal	literally, "liar". "The Dajjal" is often equated with the Christian concept of the Anti-Christ.
dhikr	mention and remembrance of Allah.
dhulm	oppression.
du'a	supplication, "private" prayer, which may be in Arabic or one's own language.
fard	obligatory.
fitnah	literally "burning" i.e. the burning that separates the dross from the pure gold; temptation or trial. Also: tribulation or tumult.
ghusl	full ablution.
Hajj	pilgrimage to Makkah.
halal	permitted, lawful.
haram	prohibited, unlawful.
haya'	modesty, bashfulness, shyness.
hijrah	migration for the sake of Allah. "The Hijrah" refers to the migration of the Prophet ﷺ from Makkah to Yathrib (Madinah).
ihsan	highest level of obedience in worship, "that you worship Allah as if you saw Him, for if you do not see Him yet He sees you" i.e. to be aware of and sincere towards Allah.
ilah	god, object of worship.

iman	trust, acceptance, affirmation *(tasdiq)*, faith, belief.
jahiliyyah	literally, "ignorance". The time before the Prophethood of Muhammad ﷺ is referred to as the Jahiliyyah or "Age of Ignorance".
jihad	striving for the sake of Allah. This may take the form of armed struggle, or it may involve other means of "fighting" for the cause of Islam. Striving to overcome one's own weaknesses and bad habits is also a form of jihad, called *jihad an-nafs.*
jinn	a race of created beings who are created from fire (whereas human beings are created from clay). Like humans, they may be Muslims or *kafirun.*
kafir (pl. *kuffar, kafirun*)	
	unbeliever. See *kufr.*
kufr	literally "covering over" and also "ingratitude". Disbelief in Allah and his signs and commandments.
makruh	disliked or disapproved of. Refers to deeds which, while not being prohibited, are strongly discouraged.
mandub	encouraged. It is equivalent to *mustahabb.*
mahdhur	forbidden.
mubah	permitted.
muru'ah	the Arabian ideal of manhood, comprising all knightly virtues, especially, manliness, valour, chivalry, generosity and a sense of honour.
mushrikun	those who associate partners with Allah; polytheists.
qada wa' qadr	Decree and destiny. *Qada'* is the decree of Allah, which cannot be changed. *Qadr* is the individual fate or destiny of each of His creatures.
Rabb	Lord; Cherisher and Sustainer.
sabr	patience, forbearance, perseverance.

Sahabah	the Companions of the Prophet Muhammad ﷺ.
Salaf	the early generations of Muslims, especially the *Sahabah* and the *Tabi'in*.
salah	prayer, i.e. the five daily prayers which are obligatory for Muslims.
sawm	fasting.
Shari'ah	Islamic law.
shukr	gratitude, thankfulness, sincere and truthful.
siddiqun	Such people are among the foremost of the followers of the Prophet ﷺ. See al-Nisa' 4:69.
surah	a chapter of the Qur'an.
Tabi'in	literally "followers", i.e. the generation of Muslims following the *Sahabah*.
taqwa	Consciousness of Allah, especially fear and awe of Him.
tawakkul	putting one's complete trust in Allah.
Ummah	nation, community. "The Ummah" is the worldwide Muslim community.
wajib	obligatory.
wali (pl. *awliya'*)	a "friend" of Allah, one whose devotion has earned him the "companionship" of Allah. It should not be translated as "saint", which is a word that denotes Christian and Hindu concepts and as such is alien to Islam. The *mu'minun* are the *awliya'* of Allah.
zahid	one who does without.
zuhd	doing without. It has degrees.